CW00767973

Downshift

About the author

Jonquil Lowe trained as an economist, worked for several years in the City as an investment analyst and is a former head of the Money Group at Consumers' Association. Jonquil now works as a freelance researcher and journalist. She writes extensively on all areas of personal finance and is author of many other books, including *Be Your Own Financial Adviser, Money M8, The Which? Guide to Giving and Inheriting, The Which? Guide to Planning Your Pension, Take Control of Your Pension* (an Action Pack), *The Which? Guide to Money in Retirement, The Which? Guide to Shares*, and, with Sara Williams, *The Lloyds-TSB Tax Guide*.

Downshift

Restore your work–life balance

Jonquil Lowe

CONSUMERS' ASSOCIATION

Which? Books are commissioned by
Consumers' Association and published by
Which? Ltd, 2 Marylebone Road, London NW1 4DF
Email:books@which.net

Distributed by The Penguin Group:
Penguin Books Ltd, 80 Strand, London WC2R 0RL

First edition July 2004

Copyright © 2004 Which? Ltd

British Library Cataloguing in Publication Data
A catalogue record for this book is available from the British Library

ISBN 0 85202 994 2

No part of this publication may be reproduced or transmitted in any form
or by any means, electronically or mechanically, including photocopying,
recording or any information storage or retrieval system, without prior
permission in writing from the publisher, nor be otherwise circulated in
any form of binding or cover other than that in which it is published and
without a similar condition being imposed on the subsequent purchaser.
This publication is not included under licences issued by the Copyright
Agency.

For a full list of Which? books, please call 0800 252100, access our
website at www.which.net, or write to Which? Books, Freepost,
PO Box 44, Hertford SG14 1SH.

Editorial and production:Robert Gray, Ian Robinson
Index:Marie Lorimer
Original cover concept by Sarah Harmer
Cover photograph by gettyimages/Chad Ehlers

Typeset by Saxon Graphics Ltd, Derby
Printed and bound by Creative Print and Design, Wales

This book provides general guidance only. Before taking action it is
advisable to seek financial and/or legal assistance.

Contents

★An asterisk next to the name of an organisation in the text indicates that its address or contact details can be found in this section.

Introduction

The UK has a reputation for having the worst long-hours culture in Europe. Research by the European Commission found that around 4 million people in the UK (about one-sixth of the workforce) currently work more than 48 hours a week, around 1.5 million toil on for more than 55 hours a week, and one person in 100 puts in more than 70 hours. These proportions are much higher than in other European Union (EU) countries where by law the working week is restricted to no more than 48 hours. Moreover, the UK is the only EU country where the number of people working long hours has actually increased over the last decade.

However, there are signs of cracks in the famous UK work ethic. Evidence suggests that one in six periods of sick leave may not be genuine but are workers 'pulling sickies', often as a reaction to stress at work. A survey of workforce commitment found loyalty on the wane for the fourth year running – high among the causes of dissatisfaction was work-life balance or, more precisely, a lack of balance as workers feel they are persistently expected to do more for less.

Little wonder then that millions are reported to be downshifting – that is, cutting back on the daily grind to find a better work–life balance. The number of part-time workers is now at an all-time high. According to a government survey, the opportunity to work flexible hours is considered to be the most valuable job perk. Recent legal changes should be making this much easier for some people. After a flurry of legislation that has had employers tearing their hair to cope with the pace of change, employees who are parents now have more rights than ever before to tip the work–life balance towards life. New mothers have the right to much longer periods of maternity leave, new fathers can take time off. Adopting parents have similar rights. Parents of young or disabled children can also take unpaid leave at other times. And, importantly, parents of children under the age of six or disabled have a new right to request flexible working – though employers do not have to agree to this if they have a sound business reason not to. It is too early to tell how much use parents will make great use of these new rights. Early surveys have shown a low level of awareness and a reluctance to exercise such rights in case the flexible worker is viewed as less committed than colleagues and, for example, passed over for promotion and training.

Although parents often have to struggle hardest to juggle the competing demands of life and work, many people who are not parents would also like more time to pursue their own interests. For example, in one government survey, over three-quarters of respondents said they would like to spend more time with friends and family. Of course, the bottom line is: the choice is yours. You can, if you want to, work less and live more. So what holds people back?

Many reasons inhibit people, such as, fear of change and the risk of damaging your career prospects. But top of the list is often money. Cutting back on work usually means you'll earn less. If you are up the hilt with a mortgage and credit card debts, you may feel you have no choice but to carry on treading the mill for long hours. Yet, if you are serious about having a better work–life balance, it may be worth sacrificing some income and you might be surprised to find that the shortfall is smaller than you had expected. Tax and National Insurance usually take a hefty slice of your earnings – if your income is much above £36,000 you could be losing 41 pence of each extra pound you earn. On top of that, you may be paying out a fair whack on travel to work, costly lunches, work clothes, and childcare. Downshifting might cut your income but, if it is also saving you all those costs, the change in your take-home pay may be very small indeed. Moreover, there are many different ways to downshift and not all involve large cuts in your immediate income – for example, you might be able to take early retirement and use a pension to supplement your earnings, or you might be lucky enough to have a skill that can command a fairly high fee. So do not assume that downshifting automatically means donning a hair shirt and living off roots. It is possible to downshift and maintain a reasonable standard of living while enjoying a much enhanced quality of life.

This book aims to help you take a good look at the financial consequences and legal aspects of shifting work down a gear in order to get some of your life back. It also encourages you to take a good look at yourself to test whether you have what it takes to make a success of downshifting and to enjoy your new life. The book is aimed at people who are prepared to go beyond the 'I'd love to if only...' stage and check out whether dreams could become reality.

There are numerous ways to downshift. You could simply be looking at containing the hours in your existing job to a sensible limit right through to quitting work altogether. This guide takes you through the options: career breaks, flexible working, part-time work, job-sharing, becoming self-employed and early retirement. It considers:

- what legal rights (where applicable) you have to downshift
- how your current income might be affected
- how your spending might change, including the implications for tax
- the steps you can take to improve your financial position, including coping with a mortgage, and
- because downshifting is a life-defining change that will affect your whole future, this book also looks at the impact on your eventual pension and what you can do now to protect it.

The book draws on the real-life experiences and examples of people who have made the shift. On the whole, our downshifters are enthusiastic and it is hard not to be inspired by them, but they do not underplay the hard work and sheer courage involved: *'I am now fulfilled and work because I enjoy it!'*; *'I am so much happier now and my family life has really improved'*; *'If there is a gap between what you are doing and what you want to do, plan a way to get there and do it.'*; *'Yes, you will be worried about the future, but plan well and then be prepared to take the risk. You could regret it if you don't.'*

Downshifting is about 'getting a life', reclaiming time for yourself, for your family, for leisure and for interests too often neglected. But a more fulfilling life means that you may well enjoy your work more too. As Chapter 1 describes, a job is not simply a source of money. It can provide stimulation, companionship and self-esteem. Often, it is not the job itself that is a problem; it is simply long hours and too much to do in too little time that cause ultimately unbearable stress and fatigue. Downshifting does not mean throwing out the good aspects of your job with the bad. Instead of life being crammed into the few hours left over after the drudgery of work, downshifting opens the prospect of a holistic approach where your work once again becomes manageable and fun so that work and life both contribute to your greater state of wellbeing.

Everyone's downshift is different. It's diversity which makes life so good. There is no single blueprint that will work for everyone, but the aim of this guide is to help you to decide if downshifting is right for you and, if so, show you how to make the leap.

This guide reflects the law and tax position in May 2004. It takes into account changes announced in the March 2004 Budget which were however still being debated by Parliament and so could be subject to some change.

Part 1

Taking stock

Chapter 1

Downshifting: dream or reality?

What is downshifting?

The term 'downshifting' was first coined in 1994 by a New York market research agency. Borrowed from motoring, the idea of moving down a gear was used to describe the phenomenon of high-flying employees opting for a lower salary in order to achieve a more fulfilling lifestyle.

The term has also been used to embrace adopting a more environmentally-friendly lifestyle or even outright rebellion against consumerism. Although these could be either goals or side effects of a downshift, they are not inevitably a part of every downshifting decision. Downshifting does not require you to emulate the 1970s sitcom *The Good Life* – unless that is what you want to do.

In this book, 'downshift' simply means any work-related step you take in order to improve your work–life balance. This includes:

- taking an extended break from your current job (see Chapter 3)
- switching to a new job or career (see Chapter 4)
- staying put but reducing the hours and stress at work (see Chapter 5)
- shifting to part-time work or job-sharing (see Chapter 5)
- telecommuting (see Chapter 6)
- quitting employment to start your own business (see Chapter 7)
- leaving paid work altogether (see Chapter 8).

The downshifters

The author and Which? Books would like to thank the real-life downshifters who have agreed to share their experiences which are described throughout this book. Their names have been changed to preserve their privacy.

Who is downshifting?

The working population of the UK comprises just under 30 million people. The research organisation, Datamonitor, published a report in 2003 suggesting that 2.6 million people in the UK (i.e. about one worker in eleven) had downshifted, up from 1.7 million five years earlier. Datamonitor predicts that the number will rise to 3.7 million by 2007. It defined downshifting as taking a cut in salary or working fewer hours. It found that the typical downshifter was in his or her 30s or 40s, mostly well-educated and with children.

But measuring downshifting is not a precise art. A more recent survey by an Australian academic, Dr Clive Hamilton, reckoned that a quarter of Britons aged 30 to 59 had downshifted over the last ten years – and a quarter of these had made the shift in the last year. In this survey, downshifting was defined as making a long-term decision which changed life in a way that involved earning less; however, it excluded people who had started their own business. Including business start-ups, the proportion downshifting would have risen to 30 per cent. Although these may seem startlingly high proportions, they are in line with results of similar research Dr Hamilton carried out into downshifting in Australia.

Dr Hamilton's research found that UK downshifting was in no way restricted to the middle-aged and wealthy. It was spread fairly evenly across all age groups and social classes, though there was a predominance of people in their 30s. Downshifters turned up in all regions but were more likely to live in the South-West, South-East or North England with fewer in Yorkshire/Humberside or London. Women were more likely to downshift than men.

Downshifters in the survey used three main methods: cutting back on the hours they worked, stopping work altogether (both particularly favoured by women) or changing career (which was more popular with men).

> *'I wanted to spend more time with my children but ended up also with more time for myself – for example, the ability to down tools on a sunny day.'*
>
> Jane, who quit a full-time job at 31 and became self-employed

Why is downshifting happening?

At a personal level, some people are finding that their main material needs have been met. They have all the toasters, fridges, TVs, hi-fis, cars, homes and holidays they want and acquiring more does not increase their happiness. They now prize non-material things, in particular time to devote to family and leisure, above acquiring more money as a means to yet more goods and services. The snag is that work takes up so much energy and so much time that there is no room in their lives for the non-material things they now crave. Downshifting is a way to achieve these new goals.

In Dr Hamilton's study (see above), the most common reason given for downshifting was to spend more time with the family. A dominant theme was a desire to regain control over time. Few said their downshifting was a backlash against materialism as such.

Table 1.1 How long does the average UK employee work?

Type of work	Average weekly hours worked in 2003 (full- and part-time workers)
Plant and machine operatives	46.1
Craft	43.1
Associate professional and technical	43.1
Professional	42.5
Managerial	41.2
Other	40.2
Personal and protective services	35.0
Clerical/secretarial	32.8
Sales	31.8
All types of work	39.6

Source: Chartered Institute of Personnel and Development, Survey report, October 2003

'If there is a gap between what you are doing and what you want to do, plan a way to go there and do it.'

John and Jenny, both in their 40s, have quit their respective jobs as an engineer and a computer programmer to train as marine biologists so they can do environmental work in warm, sunny places.

The long-hours culture

Looking at Table 1.1, you might wonder what all the fuss is about. An average working week of 39.6 hours doesn't seem so bad. But bear in mind that this is based on all workers in the survey, including those who work part-time, and the average disguises a very wide range of different experiences.

The survey for the Charter Institute of Personnel and Development (CIPD) also found that over a quarter (26 per cent) of all workers works more than 48 hours a week and one in eleven (9 per cent) works more than 60 hours a week. Moreover, there has been little or no improvement over the past five years.

To protect workers, European law aims to cap the working week at 48 hours, but the UK has an 'opt-out' which says that its workers can have longer hours provided they have voluntarily agreed to this. As a result, full-time UK workers have the longest working week in the European Union (EU) and the UK is the only EU country in which the length of the working week has risen over the last decade. It's unclear just how voluntarily UK workers have opted for this situation – see Chapter 5.

Why is downshifting happening now?

In general, the opportunity to pursue new, non-materialistic goals can be seen as a product of relative affluence. Previous generations were largely preoccupied with feeding, clothing and housing themselves. There was little money, if any, left over for luxuries, such as consumer goods or the luxury of choosing how to spend time.

Certainly, for many in current society, life is still a struggle to make ends meet – and that can be especially true if you downshift. But for most households today the struggle is more likely to be about whether to buy satellite television than how to put food on the table. It is pertinent that downshifting is fairly evenly spread across all sectors of British society and is not just the preserve of the wealthy.

Economists anticipated downshifting. Most famously, John Maynard Keynes wrote an essay in 1930 called *Economic Possibilities for our Grandchildren*. In this, he forecast the growing affluence of society over the next two generations and predicted that this would solve the economic problem which he defined as the struggle for subsistence. Having satisfied our material needs, we would be freed from the need to work so hard and so be able to pursue higher goals – what Keynes called 'the art of life'.

However, quitting work is not the inevitable outcome of increased affluence. Another renowned economist, J K Galbraith (in his book *The Affluent Society*) suggested that equally rational responses would be: to work similar hours but make work more pleasurable; and for fewer people to work, which might imply, for example, taking the very young and the very elderly out of the workforce while still ensuring that they shared in the affluence of society as a whole. In terms of downshifting, these options would translate into switching to a job you enjoyed more even if it paid less or, say, retiring early.

'I am fulfilled, have never been happier, am happily married to a teacher who works three days a week, and have lots of short holidays. Although my decision was forced on me, a complete change of lifestyle is a good thing and has completely renovated and rejuvenated me.'

Patrick, head teacher, who took early retirement at 53 because of health problems and stress and now works no more than three days a week doing work he enjoys.

Is downshifting a serious option for you?

Winning back more time to devote to the things you really enjoy is an attractive idea. But downshifting has drawbacks too. In deciding whether or not to downshift, you face two main problems:

- **being objective**. As honestly as possible, you need to identify the real benefits and real costs of downshifting. This means cutting through the romanticism that often goes with long-held ambitions and avoiding 'grass is always greener' traps
- **weighing the gains against what you lose**. (In economists' jargon, you need to do a bit of cost–benefit analysis.) This is not easy because some benefits and costs may not have a money value as such, so may be difficult to add up or balance against each other. And the weight you should give to a gain or loss is usually subjective, varying with your particular goals and circumstances. You may also have to add in the gains and losses for other people – particularly family members – who may be affected by your decision.

The subsequent chapters of this book aim to help you assess logically the pros and cons of different types of downshifting, wherever objective analysis is feasible. Inevitably though there will be some benefits and costs that only you can evaluate. A few of the main ones are briefly considered in the remainder of this chapter.

Bear in mind that downshifting is not necessarily a once-and-for-all decision. Some choose to downshift at certain stages of life – in particular, when their children are young – with the intention of resuming a fuller workload later on. In that case, it pays to plan how you will keep your work options open.

'Children are more important than money and I knew that when I was ready to return, after 10 years' experience in accounts, I would always be able to tap into this and find work.'

Lesley shifted to part-time work in accounts, turning down promotions and extra hours, in order to juggle her work with being mum to three children.

Work as a source of more than income

Your job is much more than just a source of money. Especially if you are a high-flyer, it may be a source of status among your peers and could be important to your own sense of self-esteem. You need to consider whether these factors apply to you and how important their loss would be if you are planning to change career or stop work.

Your current work, even if it is stressful, might nevertheless be challenging and stimulating. Downshifting to a less demanding job might prove boring, which can itself create stress.

The workplace as more than a place to work

In most jobs, you work with other people, so work can also be a source of friendship and camaraderie as well as a means of generating income. Would you miss human contact if, say, you opted to work from home or start your own business? On the other hand, people can sometimes be irritating or impede your development. Escaping from them could be a plus point.

Going out to work can also be important psychologically in simply giving you a change of scene and reason for getting up every morning – things you might lose if you decided, say, to work from home.

'If you feel you need to make a life change, think widely around your options and don't just go for the obvious. And, yes, you will be worried about the future, but plan well and then be prepared to take the risk. You could regret it if you don't.'

Rachel has a four-days-a-week job with flexible working and the option to work from home which allows her to spend more time with her husband, who is already retired, and her parents.

Consumerism as more than a way of meeting basic needs

Economists, including Keynes (see page 17), recognise that we have two sorts of needs:

- **absolute needs**, such as food and shelter; and
- **relative needs**, which reflect our desire to 'keep up with the Joneses'.

As UK society has become more affluent, most households can meet their basic needs. But that doesn't mean the desire to consume stops. Most households also acquire at least some non-essential items, such as televisions and microwaves, and wealthier households are of course able to acquire more of these items (see Table 1.2). Some items might not be things that you especially desire to have for themselves, but if everyone else has switched to DVDs then perhaps you might feel left behind if you don't. If the status symbols of wealth are a swimming pool and tennis court, perhaps even a non-sporty person may feel a relative need to have them.

> *'We wouldn't change our lives for the world now, because our son, Adam, gives us so much more that money DEFINITELY could not buy.'*
>
> Christine switched to part-time and home-working to spend time with her infant son.

However, you might imagine there comes a point when even relative needs are fulfilled – Keynes certainly thought that the majority of people might reach this stage. But he perhaps underestimated the ingenuity of capitalist economies to generate new things for people to desire. If people no longer demand a particular product, producers do not simply shrug and shut up shop. Usually well in advance, they will have invented something new to launch on to the market hopefully to provide a new source of profits. This has been facilitated by rapidly advancing technology which means that, almost as soon as you have acquired the latest state-of-the-art object of desire, there is a superior replacement available. Stand still and you quickly slip behind in the relativity stakes.

In today's society, satisfying relative needs seems to mean giving in to a constant pressure to consume. If the form of downshifting you choose requires you to live on a smaller income, you will probably have to turn your back on at least some of your relative needs. How do you feel about that? Some people couldn't care at all how they compare with others, especially when it comes to material possessions. For others, the perceived standing that goes with projecting a particular lifestyle or degree of wealth is important.

> *'I decided that the prospect of a good pension was not worth having a miserable working life for the next 30 years.'*
>
> Harriet, former civil servant, who now works 26 hours a week in education.

Table 1.2 Ownership by British households of selected non-essential goods in 2001

Percentage of households with:

	Up to 100	100.01 –150	150.01 –200	200.01 –250	250.01 –300	300.01 –350	350.01 –400	400.01 –450	450.01 –500	500.01 or more	All house- holds
Television											
– colour	97%	98%	99%	98%	99%	97%	98%	99%	100%	99%	98%
– black and white	1%	0%	0%	1%	0%	0%	0%	0%	0%	0%	0%
– satellite/cable/digital	27%	27%	31%	34%	40%	41%	49%	47%	50%	54%	42%
Video recorder	72%	76%	84%	87%	91%	91%	93%	96%	96%	96%	88%
CD player	59%	57%	62%	72%	81%	84%	88%	91%	89%	95%	80%
Home computer	27%	22%	29%	31%	41%	42%	50%	55%	58%	75%	50%
Access to Internet at home	20%	14%	20%	23%	27%	29%	37%	40%	46%	66%	40%
Microwave oven	77%	82%	80%	82%	85%	85%	91%	88%	90%	90%	85%
Deep freezer/fridge freezer	87%	92%	93%	92%	95%	96%	96%	95%	97%	98%	94%
Washing machine	79%	85%	89%	91%	93%	94%	94%	96%	97%	98%	92%
Tumble drier	42%	40%	44%	47%	52%	53%	52%	57%	58%	65%	54%
Dishwasher	13%	9%	13%	14%	17%	19%	21%	24%	28%	47%	28%
Telephone	94%	96%	98%	97%	99%	98%	100%	99%	99%	100%	98%
– fixed	84%	87%	91%	90%	91%	89%	94%	94%	96%	98%	93%
– mobile	49%	46%	48%	57%	68%	69%	75%	79%	81%	89%	70%
Central heating	88%	90%	90%	86%	89%	88%	91%	93%	94%	97%	92%
Car or van – more than one	11%	6%	9%	9%	13%	17%	18%	27%	29%	53%	28%

Source: Office for National Statistics

Your response to change

Downshifting to achieve a new, better status quo cannot be achieved overnight. It will inevitably involve a transitional period. This may be unsettling and its duration unpredictable. Can you cope with that?

Eventually, you will hopefully reach a new equilibrium, but any change involves risks. Later chapters of this book focus in particular on the financial risks involved. But these are not the only ones. Suppose your new, downshifted life turns out not to be the idyll you had hoped for? Are you prepared to cope with disappointments? Do you have the sort of character that can re-evaluate the options and change direction again if need be?

'However much you want to leave work and do your own thing instead, don't be surprised if you find the decision difficult to make.'

Nick took early retirement at 55 to study musical instrument making and restoration – something he had wanted to try for 30 years.

Chapter 2

Do you have what it takes?

From time to time, most people think how good it would be to cut loose from the stresses and strains of their current job and pursue a different lifestyle. Often this is just a daydream, but if you really want to turn aspiration into action, what are the factors and personal qualities which are most likely to help you succeed? There is no single, definitive list but this chapter presents a variety of ideas, many drawing on the experiences of the case studies who agreed to participate in this book.

The financial necessities

Financial viability is crucial to the success of a downshift and, along with your legal rights and duties, forms a central theme of Chapters 3 to 8. The key areas to consider are outlined below.

> *'I planned extensively and in detail, There was a huge amount to consider, decide and organise. I'd belonged to three pension schemes and had to find out exactly what I would get from each ... I did detailed monthly budgets to check whether I'd have enough money.'*
>
> Nick

Income

A downshift which involves cutting the hours you work (either in your current job or by taking a new, less demanding job), shifting to lower-paid work or stopping work altogether will inevitably reduce your earnings. You need to plan how you will cope with this. See Chapter 9 for guidance on checking the income you'll need, where the money might come from and ideas about how to boost your income.

> *'We had already paid off the mortgage on the house we were living in, in the south of England. If we were to sell that or remortgage it, we could raise some funds so finance was not an immediate concern ... The house down south has now been sold and the difference has now been banked for us to live on while completing the course. This was the ground plan at the start.'*
>
> John and Jenny

Spending

Even if income looks tight, all is not lost. You may have scope to cut your spending. In fact, your expenses may fall quite significantly directly as a result of the downshift. For example, if you are currently commuting daily to work, shifting to, say, working from home might save you thousands of pounds a year in motoring or rail costs. If you have young children, the cost of childcare to enable you to work might currently be swallowing the lion's share of your take-home pay. Chapter 9 contains more detail. Like Nick (see page 23) and Rachel (see opposite), you will probably find it helpful to draw up budgets with the aid of a spreadsheet or planner to help you work out precisely how both income and spending are likely to change. Chapter 9 contains calculators to help you do this. You can either fill in paper copies of them or use them as templates for a computer spreadsheet.

> *'Moving out of London meant we were able to buy a large house with a fairly small mortgage. That meant I had space from which to run a business. And importantly, it meant outgoings were low and I would be saving on commuting costs and other work-related expenses.'*
>
> Jane

> *'I used a planner to review my monthly expenses, building in an element for contingency and inflation. It went down to the level of building in the cost of six-weekly haircuts. I have an accountant so asked for his assessment of what my net income would be on a four-day-a-week basis. On paper, this looked to be just enough to cover all my projected expenses but meant cutting back severely on clothes, books, meals out and other treats.'*
>
> Rachel

Savings

If your downshift is temporary (for example, a year's career break in order to travel) or involves some upfront costs (say, while you set up your own business or fund retraining), you may be able to plan ahead and save enough money to tide you over. Chapter 9 includes suggestions on how to invest your savings if you need them to produce an income.

Borrowing

If you need temporary income or face initial costs, you may have to resort to borrowing. Try not to do this unless you have a sound plan for how you will repay the debts. And try to borrow in a cost-effective way. Table 2.1 ranks the main types of borrowing in order of typical cost.

If you have a mortgage, it is vital that you are able to keep up the repayments on this after your downshift. Chapter 10 has guidance on how to keep your mortgage under control and information about renting and other financial aspects of housing.

> *'Sort out your finances. Get rid of any debt you can, take advantage of all the special offers on mortgages, utilities etc. so you can live as cheaply as possible.'*
>
> Harriet

Table 2.1   Cost of main types of borrowing

Type of borrowing	Cost in April 2004 (APR)	Comments
Unauthorised overdraft	up to 41.2%	Most expensive, best avoided
Store card	up to 31.9%	Costly, best avoided
Credit card	up to 24.9%	Huge variation in cost. Shop around for a cheap card. Can be good value for short-term borrowing
Arranged overdraft	up to 19.56%	Likely to be for a limited period only
Personal loan	up to 17.8%	Likely to be cheaper than a credit card for longer-term borrowing. Shop around – you do not need to go to your current bank
Credit union loan	up to 12.68%	Credit unions are neighbourhood or workplace savings and loans groups run by savers and borrowers themselves
Mortgage (standard variable rate)	up to 6.89%	Secured against your home, so you could lose your home if you fail to keep up the repayments
Student loan	No interest rate as such. Outstanding loan increases in line with inflation (currently around 2.5% a year)	Available to university students

Sources: Moneyfacts, Department for Education and Skills

Personal qualities

Ambition or goals

Don't just associate ambition with a high-flying traditional career. It can be a desire to fulfil a childhood dream or gain a new skill. Merely being dissatisfied with your current lifestyle is not enough to make a downshift happen. You need to have some alternative in mind. Not everyone has a long-held ambition but, if you do, this may well be the target of your downshift.

> '*I wanted to be a caring, nurturing mother and give my children a good grounding before they entered school life. I believe I have achieved this.*'
>
> Lesley

> '*I ... enrolled as a mature student on a three-year full-time course in musical instrument making and restoration – something I had wanted to have a go at for 30 years.*'
>
> Nick

Interests

If you don't have a specific ambition, several of the case studies we talked to strongly recommended that you build your new life around existing interests. Whether this is feasible will depend on the type of interests you have and how dependent you will be on an income from them. Your interests must be capable of being turned into something that people want to buy. Suitable interests might involve art- or craft-based skills, such as pottery, silk-screen printing, wood-turning, or jewellery-making. Or maybe you are an enthusiastic gardener and could develop some niche, such as growing and selling herbs or turning dried flowers into pot pourri. You might have more intellectual interests and be able to design websites or offer research skills, say, tracing family histories.

Developing an existing interest will not be right for everyone. You might want to try something completely new. But sticking with existing interests has some advantages:

- you are likely to have a fair idea of what your new line of work involves and what opportunities exist
- there is a good chance that you will enjoy the new work as much as you had hoped, and less risk of falling into the 'grass is greener' trap
- you might be able to draw on existing skills rather than retraining. This in turn can mean less pressure on your finances.

> '*Follow your interests as fully as you can ... My genealogical work arose from an interest during my convalescence. My educational work developed from requests by acquaintances and friends through word of mouth.*'
>
> Patrick

> '*As we had always been interested in the marine environment through diving holidays abroad and diving with a marine biologist, who introduced us to a number of interesting facts and sights on and under the sea, we decided that we would look into this further.*'
>
> John and Jenny

Imagination

A drawback to pursuing existing interests or adapting your present line of work is that you might miss the opportunity to try something completely different.

Even if you eventually settle on a change that is not too dramatic, it is worth having a 'brainstorming session' early in your downshift planning where you let your imagination fly. If you find yourself drawn to some unexpected and novel ideas, it may be worth investigating them further to see whether there are viable options for you either directly or indirectly linked to this new direction.

> '*One friend has been in much the same position that I was* [see Rachel's story on page 90], *but the effect on her was worse. Knowing what I did, she came to talk and we discussed options. It took her a while to stop thinking of taking another job which offered her more of the same. But after things reached a crisis point, she too has gone out and added to her qualifications and launched herself on a portfolio career* (doing several different types of work all part-time) *which she is in control of and where she does the things she gets something back from.*'
>
> Rachel

Courage

Change is often unsettling. Making a major change that potentially affects every aspect of your lifestyle and finances may well seem daunting. It is perfectly natural to approach a downshift with some trepidation, but if you're confident the goals are worth having and that financially the planned change is viable, don't be put off. You need to be prepared to take some risk, but you should not be rash. Like an entrepreneur, your aim is to take only *calculated* risks not to rush blindly in. So take the time to gather the information you need to figure out what sort of risks are involved and how likely they are to materialise. Consider what you can do to minimise or eliminate risks that seem too high or unnecessary. If you still feel unsure, bear in mind that there are risks too in preserving the status quo. Depending on your reasons for downshifting, the risks of doing nothing could be damaging to your mental health, family relationships, and so on.

'Even though I was doing calculations and budgets which showed that I could implement all my plans and I'd have plenty of money to live on, I found it very hard to actually make the decision to chuck the job. It made me realise how institutionalised I'd become after working for 34 years. I felt as though it was a really big and risky step to take, as if into the unknown.'

Nick

'Yes, you will be worried but plan well and then be prepared to take the risk.'

Rachel

Determination and drive

It is not just making the initial leap that may be hard. For a variety of reasons, maintaining your new lifestyle can also be quite a challenge. For example, one case study cited the problem of part-time workers not being treated on a par with full-timers. Although the law requires equal treatment in tangible ways (see page 81), you might still find yourself affected by negative attitudes from bosses and colleagues that do not amount to a breach of law but are nevertheless unsettling. So, if you work part-time, you might feel you have to prove yourself and demonstrate your worth to others.

> *'When you work part-time, people don't see you as committed to work as much as full-timers and yet I have less time off work sick than full-time staff. I feel awkward if I have to take an unexpected day off if the children are sick, say. Because of this I make myself work even if I'm sick ... I push myself harder than some full-time staff for fear of losing my job.'*
>
> Lesley

Another individual, who had become self-employed, raised the not uncommon problem of containing a successful business. On the one hand, you may choose self-employment in order to work shorter hours and reduce stress; on the other, you cannot afford to turn away so much work that you lose clients. Keeping your business at the optimum size can be something of a balancing act.

> *'For the past two months, it is apparent that I have passed a critical point and word of mouth now delivers more work than I wish to take on. This is becoming a new problem but a welcome one!'*
>
> Patrick

Self-belief

It is essential that you believe in yourself and in your ability to make your downshift happen. This may seem obvious if you are choosing to downshift, but it is more tricky if your downshift is involuntary.

Redundancy, having to stop work because of illness, or even stopping work when you have a child, can mean you suddenly find yourself pitched into a new lifestyle. You may have strongly identified yourself and your self-worth through your work and job status, in which case your initial reaction might be depression, anger, dissatisfaction and a whole host of other negative feelings. Once you have come to terms with the change, hopefully you will be able to see positive aspects too and open yourself to the prospect of new opportunities.

> 'Ultimately do what you want – even if it doesn't quite work out as you hoped. Doing different, more rewarding work can lead to new opportunities and new avenues you might not have thought of before.'
>
> Harriet
>
> 'Don't assume you are finished.'
>
> Patrick

Self-sufficiency

If your downshift involves working from home, either as an employee (say, a teleworker) or running your own business, don't overlook the fact that you are likely to be working on your own a lot of the time. This is a big change if you have been used to working with other people.

Aspects you might miss include: companionship, the opportunity to meet new people and make new friends, ad hoc chats, the sparking of new ideas through talks with colleagues, and working as part of a team. For you, these might not be important – in fact, you might even relish being able to get on with your work without interruption. Alternatively, you might find that you can use other areas of your life to provide the aspects missing in your working life. But, for some people, working from home becomes too lonely and their initial enthusiasm does not last.

> 'At times the isolation of working from home has been a problem but I countered this by getting involved in community events for several years, for example, becoming a town councillor and starting a local festival. This enabled me to work with other people and so filled the gap to some extent.'
>
> Jane
>
> 'Working from home is not for everyone as you are more on your own, but I find it suits me. I had wondered if I might miss seeing my new colleagues, but I use days when I am in the office to catch up with news and socialise and email keeps us in touch too.'
>
> Rachel

Planning skills

If a downshift is thrust upon you through, say, redundancy or ill-ness, you inevitably do not have much scope for planning ahead – at least regarding your immediate future. But longer term, and if you are choosing voluntarily to downshift, planning seems to pay off. This was a recurrent theme with our case studies.

> *'I had been thinking for some time of going part-time and moving to a job which gave me a better work-life balance. I had attended a career review course a few years earlier to think through the options. This helped me identify the experience and qualifications I wanted to obtain before making a substantial shift towards the type of work I had identified as wanting to move to. One which would enable me to use the skills I get most job satisfaction from, working part time, having more control over my working life and ultimately having the option of going into self-employment.'*
>
> Rachel
>
> *'I spent a huge amount of time considering the financial implica-tions. Coming from a background where I lived with an alcoholic mother who never had any money, I hated the idea of not having enough money to live on.'*
>
> Harriet
>
> *'Plan thoroughly and do the sums objectively and, if it works on paper, go for it. If you're taking early retirement, ignore all the received 'facts' you hear about pensions. If you do the sums, you may find that these facts are all wrong in your case.'*
>
> Nick
>
> *'Try to see if the outside world has a demand for what you can offer, but only on a small scale initially, building up experience until you are confident you can cope.'*
>
> Patrick

'The downshift was planned to the extent that we had been looking at a review of life at 40. (Any good business plan should have a "review strategy" at regular intervals and this was a major one.) We looked at a number of options, such as straightforward emigration and carrying on with similar work elsewhere, staying put or looking at something different. Staying put was ruled out and after lots of "what I would like to do" lists (from both of us separately then looking for common objectives), emigration looked a good bet. Unfortunately, we are considered too old to simply emigrate without jobs to go to and the only jobs we could get on current qualifications would be doing the things we had decided to get away from. Next choice was to retrain ...'

John and Jenny

Flexibility

However organised you are, your downshift will not necessarily run according to plan. As far as possible, it pays to anticipate possible problems and think in advance how you might deal with them. For example:

- if you switch career, what will you do if you don't like the new work after all? Can you find another outlet for your skills still within your chosen downshifted area? Are you prepared to switch back to your old career? Is there a further new area you would want to explore?
- if you need to study or train for something new, suppose you can't get on to the course you want, or you fail to get the qualification, or you can't get a job at the end of it? Is there an alternative course? Can you retake exams? Are there other related jobs that would be an acceptable alternative?
- if you try to make a living out of an existing interest or hobby, what will you do if you can't sell enough? Do you simply need to pep up your marketing? Or do you have a product or service that really is not in demand? Can you use the same interest in a different way to produce some other goods or service?

- if you start your own business, what if it fails? Would you be able to return to your previous work? Is there another career you could turn to? Alternatively, what will you do if the business is a runaway success and takes up more and more of your time? Would you be prepared to turn down customers in order to keep the business artificially small? Or could you put the downshift on hold and give more to the business instead? Would it be feasible to maintain your downshift by, say, taking on staff to do some of the work for you?

- if you take a complete career break, say, to spend time with a young family, suppose you miss the stimulation of work? Could you perhaps work part-time instead?

- what if your finances don't pan out as expected? For example, suppose your pension or a redundancy package is less than expected? Suppose you're reliant on selling your home but it doesn't sell or property prices collapse? Suppose you have borrowed and interest rates soar? Can you raise money in other ways? From the outset is it worth borrowing at a fixed rate so that you know your payments will not change if interest rates rise? What about a flexible mortgage to give you some leeway if you hit a rough patch? Can you cut your spending?

You should also consider how long you will give yourself to make a success of your downshift. For example, if you are starting your own business, how long will you allow to build up a customer base and to start turning in a reasonable profit? If you have switched to another career, when do you plan to take stock and decide whether it is fulfilling your expectations regarding work-life balance, financial security and overall happiness? The time you allow yourself depends on:

- **the type of downshift**, for example, you will need longer if you are retraining or starting a business than if you are simply stepping down from full-time to part-time work. And working in a new field may be stressful at the start but should become less so as you gain expertise, but the time this takes will vary with the depth of new skills you need to acquire

- **how crucial it is that you make money** from your downshifted work. This may be less important if you have other resources, such as an early retirement pension, another job or a working spouse or partner, in which case you may be able to give the venture longer to get off the ground.

> '*Do research into your chosen career path and have a second option in case your first doesn't work out ... I attended my PGCE* [Post Graduate Certificate of Education] *interview and then learnt that I had NOT been successful. I didn't know what to do. I hadn't even thought about what I would do if I didn't get on to the course. This was a stressful time.*'
>
> Harriet
>
> '*Plan what you want to do and go for it, but be flexible in the way you go about it. Don't just think: I am at A and want to go to B. You may need some intermediate steps to get there (like we bought the second house to stay in up north ... before committing to the move and selling up down south ...).*'
>
> John and Jenny

An appetite for hard work

Although you may be downshifting to reduce the demands of work on your time, initially at least you may need to put in some intensive effort.

Imagine if your downshift were a project you had been given to do at work, with serious consequences and big budget implications. You'd need to consider all the angles, do the research, put together a plan for implementation, see it through all the critical stages, appraise progress at regular intervals. Your life is the biggest project you will ever undertake, so it is worth a bit of effort to make sure your change of direction is the right one.

> '*It may sound ridiculous but it was an intense seven-month project as there was so much to sort out and difficult and important decisions to make. I don't think I've ever worked so hard in my life – I ran on adrenalin and coffee for seven months. But I enjoyed it as I knew I was doing it entirely for myself and my future life.*'
>
> Nick

Lack of materialism

Perhaps it's a truism to say that downshifters are less materialist than most people. After all, they are willing to forsake the rewards of work (usually financial) in order to pursue non-monetary goals in life (often the acquisition of more time). But it is worth pointing out that if your hobbies tend to be expensive or you like fine living you might find it hard to take the financial sacrifice that many downshifts imply.

If you have a partner, or other family who will be affected by your downshift, they may have to share your financial fortunes. Are they as non-materialistic as you?

> *'My motives were … the realisation that I didn't want to be rich. I just wanted to have enough money to spend my time doing things I wanted to do, regardless of whether they earned me money or not.'*
>
> Nick
>
> *'Is there such a thing as a serial downshifter? Some years before this present change, I had given up a potentially very lucrative job in the City. I felt it was just not worth selling my soul for money. It was important to me that I could feel my work was useful – and I really felt like quite a parasite working in stockbroking – so I was happy to trade a pay cut for greater job satisfaction.'*
>
> Jane

Catalyst or opportunity

Financial wherewithal and personal characteristics alone do not necessarily make a downshifter. Another factor is often a specific opportunity or catalyst that triggers the decision (or need) to downshift.

This might happen when you reach a certain stage of life – for example, the birth of a child, your children leaving home, or an elderly relative needing care. The trigger might be worsening problems at work. In the case of involuntary downshifting, the 'opportunity' is forced on you by, say, redundancy or ill health.

'In the event, the need to change jobs was accelerated by a major change at work. This led to hugely increased pressures and very long hours. What started as tiredness very quickly turned to stress, at a level which was undermining my health. I was determined not to 'give in' to this and developed my own set of 'anti-stress' techniques to help me cope. But I knew that I had to remove myself from the cause of the stress – the job – and actively started looking for a new one. One which would enable me to get as close to the goals I had identified as I could.'

Rachel

'The opportunity arose because: I was separated, so only had myself to consider; my younger daughter had just finished university so I no longer had any children to support and could manage on a lower income; and I had belonged to three better-than-average pension schemes ... and so, with lower costs, I found I could afford to take early retirement.'

Nick

'I was a secondary head teacher who had minor strokes and heart problems combined with work-related stress. My downshift was forced upon me so I did no planning.'

Patrick

'The day jobs were no longer challenging and ageism and the "qualifications culture" were both preventing any serious advancement. Where I was, there was a need to possess a degree (in almost any subject, relevant to the work or not) to demonstrate that there were a couple of brain cells in there somewhere and years of experience in the job were not being counted for much at all. For the wife's work in mainframe computing, the bubble burst after all the year 2000 hype and that, coupled with Inland Revenue regulation IR35 [see page 122], meant that the freedom to contract and enjoy the fruits of your labour had taken a significant knock as well as there being less work available.'

John and Jenny

> *'We worked out that I would be going to work simply to pay Adam's nursery fees if I went back to work full-time.'*
>
> Christine

Support

Finally, however much you are committed to downshifting, do you have the support of the people that matter to you?

Most importantly, your downshift is likely to affect the people who live with you. For example, if you will be bringing in less money, they may have to either tighten their belts or be prepared to bring in extra income. If you plan to spend more time with them, they may also need to plan how they can spend more time with you. You may be looking forward to being at home all day, but will your spouse or partner be so happy about that? If you are taking a career break to, say, travel, will your partner or family come too? If not, will they be happy to cope without you for a while? Ideally, you should discuss your ideas with your family at an early stage and – especially where a husband, wife or partner is concerned – share the decision-making with them.

Family members who are not part of your household, friends and colleagues might all have something to say about what you are up to. Their encouragement may be welcome. But, if they are not directly affected by your downshift, be wary of being too heavily influenced by their views – positive or negative. At the end of the day, it's your work–life balance and your decision.

That said, friends and others who have relevant experience can be a helpful source of information, advising on computer systems, suggesting useful outlets for something you intend to make or just sharing their own experiences over a cup of tea. In other areas, consider getting professional advice, for example, from an independent financial adviser (IFA)★ or accountant★ regarding financial planning, from a careers service★ if you are planning a career switch, or from Business Link★ if you are considering setting up your own business. See Chapter 3 to 8 for more about sources of information.

'My husband has been hugely supportive throughout this whole process. Without him, I would still be stuck in a job I hated. He gave me the confidence to believe in myself and my abilities (something that six years of Ministry of Defence work had stripped away).'

Harriet

'It took me four months of planning before I made the decision and told everyone what I was doing. I actually got a very positive response from almost everyone and after that I was fine.'

Nick

'Do your homework – look for help and take what's offered; don't be afraid to ask others for advice and help.'

John and Jenny

'Once YOU have decided what YOU want to do, then do it – I had a number of people telling me I was mad when I first handed in my resignation but within a week or so they were saying they wished they could do it.'

John and Jenny

Checklist: do you have what it takes?

Factor	Is it important for the type of downshifting you intend?		Do you have this factor?	
Financial resources				
Enough income	Yes ☐	No ☐	Yes ☐	No ☐
Control over your spending	Yes ☐	No ☐	Yes ☐	No ☐
Savings you can use	Yes ☐	No ☐	Yes ☐	No ☐
Borrowing that you know how you will repay	Yes ☐	No ☐	Yes ☐	No ☐
Other financial resources	Yes ☐	No ☐	Yes ☐	No ☐
Personal resources				
Ambition/specific goals	Yes ☐	No ☐	Yes ☐	No ☐
Interests you can develop	Yes ☐	No ☐	Yes ☐	No ☐
Imagination	Yes ☐	No ☐	Yes ☐	No ☐
Courage	Yes ☐	No ☐	Yes ☐	No ☐
Determination/drive	Yes ☐	No ☐	Yes ☐	No ☐
Self-belief	Yes ☐	No ☐	Yes ☐	No ☐
Self-sufficiency	Yes ☐	No ☐	Yes ☐	No ☐
Planning skills	Yes ☐	No ☐	Yes ☐	No ☐
Flexibility	Yes ☐	No ☐	Yes ☐	No ☐
An appetite for hard work	Yes ☐	No ☐	Yes ☐	No ☐
Lack of materialism	Yes ☐	No ☐	Yes ☐	No ☐
Other resources				
Opportunity	Yes ☐	No ☐	Yes ☐	No ☐
Support from immediate family	Yes ☐	No ☐	Yes ☐	No ☐
Reliable sources of help and information	Yes ☐	No ☐	Yes ☐	No ☐

Part 2

Different ways to downshift

Chapter 3

Taking a career break

A career break involves a temporary downshift, for example, while you travel, study or spend time with young children. It might involve a complete break from work or juggling time off with a less demanding part-time job. Your main concerns are likely to be:

- your prospects or right to return to work after the break
- your income during the break
- the impact on your eventual pension.

Probably the most common career break is a parent – typically the mother – taking time off to care for a new baby or young child. The law gives parents the right to a certain amount of paid or unpaid leave and recently there have been important improvements to these rights – see pages 45–47.

There are many other motives for considering a career break. For example, you might want to take stock if you are facing a mid-life crisis, to recharge your batteries if you feeling physically or mentally drained, to escape from stress for a while, or to upgrade your skills by taking a full-time course, perhaps an MBA. You might have more hedonistic reasons for a break, such as travelling the world, or going on an extended honeymoon. Whatever the motive or circumstances of your break, the law does not usually give you either the right to such a break or the right to return to the same job, but your employer might voluntarily operate a career break scheme or be willing to consider your request for an extended break – see page 47.

Christine's story

Christine lives with her husband, Gregory, and 14-month-old son, Adam. She decided to take a break from full-time work to spend time with her son during his early years. *'I had a problem pregnancy and was signed off sick for four months, which gave me plenty of time to think about what we were going to do once Adam was born. I went back to work part-time when Adam was three months old, because we worked out that I would be going to work simply to pay his nursery fees if I went back full-time. So I got a job in Tesco's working three evenings a week (5pm to 10pm) and Saturday mornings (7am to midday). I can spend the rest of my time at home with my son.'*

Your prospects if you quit for a while

If you resign from your current job in order to take a break, it is worth considering what you can do during the break to make it easier when you want to return to work. For example, you might consider subscribing to journals that will keep you up to date with developments in your field, from time to time you could go on relevant training courses, maybe you could study part-time or through distance learning for relevant qualifications, or you could perhaps take on some work – say, a few hours a week – just to keep your hand in.

If you are currently self-employed and plan to take a break, bear in mind that your customers or clients will have to find alternative suppliers and will not necessarily come back to you if you decide to start up the same business again. If that is your aim, it might be that reducing your hours rather than stopping altogether would be a more viable option.

'Don't leave it too long to get back to your chosen career path or else it will be too difficult to get back in. I left accounts work ... then eventually picked up my career doing temporary work.'

Lesley

'I stopped work completely for about nine months just before my oldest child started school because I felt both children needed more attention from me at that stage. Looking back, it was a high-risk thing to do. I was very lucky that, when I realised I really did need a work–life balance, not simply no work at all, my clients were happy to resume putting business my way. The business could so easily have folded altogether as a result of that break.'

Jane

Your employment rights if you take a break

Parents' rights to a break

Since April 2003, parents who are employees have acquired improved rights to time off work when a child is born or they first adopt. These rights apply equally to part-time as well as full-time employees. Parents of young or disabled children also have new rights to request flexible working – see Chapter 5.

New mothers

Women are now entitled to more generous maternity leave. Regardless of how short a time you have worked for your current employer, you are entitled to 26 weeks' ordinary maternity leave and this will normally be paid leave. Apart from pay, all your other terms and conditions continue during your ordinary leave. For example, you still build up holiday entitlement and continue to benefit from perks such as a company car, and so on.

Provided you have worked continuously for your employer for at least 26 weeks up to the fifteenth week before the baby is due, you can choose to take up to a further 26 weeks' additional maternity leave running straight on from your ordinary leave (making a break of up to 52 weeks altogether). Additional leave is usually unpaid, unless your employment contract states otherwise. Some terms and conditions continue during additional leave – for example, right to notice if your job ends, right to redundancy pay – but what other terms if any continue depends on your particular contract of employment or whatever you can negotiate with your employer.

You have the right to return at the end of your ordinary or additional leave to the same job and on the same terms as applied before the leave started. You are entitled to benefit from any general pay increases or improvements in terms that have been introduced while you were away.

Usually, you must tell your employer by the end of the fifteenth week before your child is due that you intend to take maternity leave. You can then take the full 52 weeks without giving any further notice. If you want to come back early, you must give your employer 28 days' notice of your return.

Ordinary maternity leave counts as part of your continuous employment, and so counts towards employment rights such as redundancy pay. Additional maternity leave does not count, but your service immediately before and after the additional leave are joined together and count as continuous service. See page 52 for what happens to pension rights in an occupational scheme.

You can be made redundant while on maternity leave but not for any reason connected with your pregnancy or becoming a parent (or for any other reason that would amount to discrimination on the grounds of sex or your marital status). If you are made redundant, you must be given a written statement of the reason for your redundancy.

Other new parents

Employees also have a right to take leave if they newly adopt a child. This leave and the rights associated with it are very similar to the maternity leave described above. The main exception is that to be eligible even for ordinary adoption leave you must have worked continuously for your employer for at least 26 weeks up to the qualifying week (which is the week you are notified that you have been matched to a child). You can then take up to 26 weeks' ordinary leave followed, if you choose, by a further 26 weeks' additional leave. You might qualify for statutory adoption pay (see page 50) during the first 26 weeks.

Where a couple adopt, only one of them can claim adoption leave. However, the other might be able to claim paternity leave (even if in this case the partner is a woman).

Paternity leave can be claimed by the biological father of a new baby, the husband or partner of a mother having a new baby, or the husband or partner (including a same-sex partner) of an adopting parent. The maximum leave is two weeks, which must be used either for caring for the child or helping the new parent.

To be eligible for paternity leave, you must have worked for 26 weeks with the same employer up to the qualifying week. You might also qualify for statutory paternity pay (see page 50).

A parent of a child under six or a disabled child and who has been employed continuously by the same employer for at least a year also has the right to take unpaid paternal leave – for up to 13 weeks per child during a child's first five years, or 18 weeks up to age 18 in the case of a disabled child. You do not have to take the leave all in one go. You remain employed while on leave and have the right to return to the same job (or in some cases a similar job).

Other or longer breaks

There are many circumstances other than those described above when you might want to take a career break – in other words, unpaid leave with a view to returning to the same job or same employer afterwards. However, you generally do not have any legal right to take either a career break for non-family-related reasons or, if family-related, for longer than the breaks described above. However, some employers do offer a formal career break scheme. If yours doesn't, you might be able to negotiate some arrangement, but it is important that both you and your employer are clear about the contractual details. For example, you could follow the provisions that might be found in a typical formal career break scheme.

A scheme might be restricted to certain types of career break – for example, to care for children or an elderly relative or to study relevant qualifications – or might be open for any purpose.

Whether you use a formal scheme or an informal arrangement, a key area that it is essential to be clear on is the impact on your continuity of employment. Some important employment rights – for example, to protection against unfair dismissal and concerning redundancy pay – depend on how long you have been in continuous employment with your current employer. And the way your break is treated will also affect any occupational pension (see page 52).

Many formal schemes require you actually to resign from your job, though others do not. Even if you have to resign, it does not necessarily follow that the continuity of your employment will be broken, though this is likely if the situation is similar to that considered in a tribunal case in 2002 (see Box opposite). If you do not have to resign, there is no law specifically saying what must happen regarding continuity, so make sure that your employer explains to you at the outset how the contract is intended to work.

Typical features of a career break scheme are:

- the break must last a minimum period, say six months
- the break must be no longer than a maximum period, say five years
- your employer either promises you your job back (or one of a similar grade) when you return – sometimes called a 're-entry scheme' – or does not give an absolute promise but agrees to make every effort to re-employ you – called a 'reservist scheme'
- your employer usually has the right to cancel the promise or agreement on giving you, say, three months' notice
- you are required to give notice to your employer when you intend to return to work or wish to pull out of the scheme
- while on the break, you might be barred from doing any paid work for another employer. Alternatively, you might require consent from your employer before you can do so
- you are required to keep in touch with work, usually by continuing to do at least a minimum amount of work – say, two weeks every year. You will probably also be invited to various work functions. You might be assigned a mentor who keeps you abreast of the work
- apart from the periods you are required or invited to go back in to work, your pay stops.

A career break scheme must be open to part-time employees as well as full-time workers, but casual and contract employees are unlikely to be included.

Sparks fly over career break

In 2002, an important case concerning a career break came before an employment tribunal. Ms Curr had worked for Marks & Spencer since 1973. In 1990, by which time she was a manager, she started a four-year break to spend time looking after her family. Marks & Spencer required her to resign from her job and promised her an equivalent job on her return. During the break, she had to work for Marks & Spencer for two weeks a year and had to seek the firm's approval before doing paid work for anyone else.

She came back in 1994 but, a little over four years later, in 1999, Marks & Spencer made her redundant. Marks & Spencer offered Ms Curr redundancy pay based on four years' service. Ms Curr challenged this, claiming it should be based on 25 years back to 1973.

Initially, the employment tribunal found for Ms Curr but the Court of Appeal reversed that decision. While the Appeal Court felt that Marks & Spencer did have some moral obligation towards Ms Curr, it found that the obligations placed on each party following the resignation and during the career break did not amount to a contract of employment and so the continuity of employment had been broken. Therefore, for the purpose of working out redundancy pay, the contract of employment started in 1994.

Financial aspects of taking a career break

Impact on your income

If you are a parent, you might qualify for some ongoing pay or state benefits during your break, at least for a limited period. In other cases and if you are a parent wanting to take more time off than your legal rights allow, a break in your career is likely to mean a break in your income too.

New parents

Most employed women taking ordinary maternity leave qualify for statutory maternity pay (SMP). It is payable for a total of 26 weeks. For the first six weeks, this is paid at a rate of 90 per cent of your weekly earnings averaged over the eight weeks before what is known as the 'qualifying week'. The qualifying week is the fifteenth week before your baby is due. Over the following 20 weeks, you get either 90 per cent of your average pay or £102.80 a week (in 2004–5) whichever is lower. Your employer might operate its own maternity scheme which pays you more than SMP.

To be eligible for SMP, you must have worked continuously for your employer for at least 26 weeks up to the qualifying week, have average earnings over the eight-week period of at least the lower earnings limit (£79 a week in 2004–5) and give your employer notice that you will be claiming SMP.

SMP and any payments from your employer's own maternity scheme are taxable like ordinary pay and paid to you by your employer in the same way as your normal salary through the PAYE system with tax and National Insurance already deducted.

If you are not eligible for SMP, you might be able to claim maternity allowance instead (also payable at £102.80 a week in 2004–5, but maternity allowance is a tax-free state benefit). Maternity allowance may also be available if you are self-employed.

If you newly adopt a child, you may be able to claim statutory adoption pay (SAP) which works in a very similar way to SMP and is paid at the same rates as SMP for a maximum of 26 weeks.

Statutory Paternity Pay is also paid at the lower of 90 per cent of average pay or £102.80 a week in 2004–5 but for only a maximum of two weeks. As with SMP, to be eligible you must have worked continuously for your employer for at least 26 weeks up to the qualifying week, have average earnings over the eight-week period of at least the lower earnings limit (£79 a week in 2004–5) and give your employer notice that you will be claiming SPP.

Both SAP and SPP are taxable and paid like your normal pay through PAYE with tax and National Insurance contributions already deducted.

In all cases, the statutory pay outlined above is the minimum you must get if eligible. Your employer might operate a more generous scheme.

Other career breaks

If you are taking a career break for non-family reasons or you are a parent taking off longer than the leave allowed by law, you are unlikely to be eligible for any ongoing regular pay – though, under a formal career break scheme, you may be required to do, say, two weeks paid work with your employer per year and could be offered the opportunity to do more if your employer is short-staffed. But, in general, you will need to plan to fund a career break in some other way than through income. Possible sources of funding might be:

- savings you have built up in advance of taking the break
- borrowing during your career break. If you adopt this course, make sure you have a clear strategy for repaying the loan
- sale of assets. For example, you might trade down to a smaller home and live off the money released. Or you might have some valuables – say, antiques – that you could sell to raise the money you need.

Impact on your spending

Taking a career break will have a big impact on your spending during the period of the break. For example, you will save on travel-to-work costs and, where you are taking the break to care for young children, you will probably be saving on the costs of childcare that you would need to pay for in order to work. Particularly in the case of childcare, the savings could be enough to largely offset the loss of income.

However, you'll usually have extra costs too depending on the reason for your career break. For example, if you will be studying, you may have the costs of tuition fees, books, travel to college, and so on. (There is more information about the income and spending implications of being a mature student in Chapter 4 – see pages 66 and 70.) If you are travelling around the world, you'll have the cost of fares, accommodation, and so on. It is impossible to be specific about the costs you will face because there are so many different ways in which you could use a career break. Chapter 9 will help you focus on the spending needs that you are likely to experience during your particular career break.

Impact on your pension

State pension

If you are a new parent receiving SMP, SAP or SPP, you will still be building up your National Insurance record and so a limited break should not have any impact on your state basic pension but might affect your state second pension – see Chapter 12. Even when the benefits stop, you may be eligible for home responsibilities protection (see page 220) which may help to protect your state pensions.

In other cases, a career break will usually mean a gap in your National Insurance contribution record. This may cause a reduction in your eventual state basic pension and you will stop building up state second pension during the break. There is nothing you can do about the state second pension, but it might be worth paying voluntary Class 3 National Insurance contributions to protect your basic pension rights – see pages 204 and 225.

Occupational pension

If you are taking ordinary maternity leave, ordinary adoption leave, paternity leave, or paternal leave on or after 6 April 2003, your occupational pension rights are protected. Your employer must carry on paying contributions on your behalf as if you were continuing to receive your normal pay. But any contributions you are required to make will be based on your actual pay during the leave. The period of ordinary leave will count as part of your continuous service.

If you started additional maternity or adoption leave (or paternal leave before 6 April 2003), the leave period does not have to be counted as part of your continuous service, but the periods immediately before and after the leave are joined together to create a continuous period for pension purposes. What happens beyond that depends on the particular rules of your scheme.

Where you take a career break for other reasons, there is no specific protection regarding your pension. You will need to consult your employer and the rules of the pension scheme to check how your pension might be treated in your particular case. It is extremely unlikely that the career break itself will be counted as part of your continuous service, but ideally you would hope that the periods of work immediately before and after the break will be joined together and treated as a continuous period for pension purposes. In the worst scenario, you will be treated as leaving the pension scheme at the start of your break with any subsequent membership being treated as a separate period of membership.

Personal pension

If you stop paying into a personal pension during a career break, this will reduce your eventual pension beyond what it would otherwise have been. Consider making extra payments to catch up once you return to work.

Further information

For more information about your statutory rights to leave and pay if you are a parent, see the free booklets from the Department of Trade and Industry (DTI)* listed in Table 3.1.

For information about any career break scheme at work, contact your human resources (personnel) department.

For details about the rules of your employer's occupational pension scheme, talk to your pensions administrator, who is usually based in the human resources department.

Table 3.1   Useful DTI booklets

Reference number	Title
PL958	*Maternity rights: a guide for employers and employees*
PL517	*Working fathers: rights to paternity leave and pay*
PL518	*Adoptive parents: rights to leave and pay when a child is placed for adoption in the UK*
PL509	*Parental leave: detailed guidance for employers and employees*

Chapter 4

Changing jobs or career

A complete switch of job or career can be a way of improving your quality of life, particularly if it involves less stress, less overtime and maybe fulfilling a long-held ambition to develop particular skills or work in a particular field.

But, of all the types of downshifting, this is perhaps the most risky. You need to view your options with a strong dose of reality. Switching may involve a lower income and reduced status (especially if you move from being an expert in one field to a novice in your new career). You may be swapping one set of stress inducers for another – different but just as intolerable. You may have to support yourself through a lengthy period of retraining and, at the end of that, you might find it hard to get the job you want. You might discover that you are not as good at your new job as you had expected or that it is not as challenging or as interesting as you had hoped. You should brace yourself against possible disappointments and be flexible if your plans don't go as intended.

This is an intensely personal kind of downshifting. Just because it works for one person, it does not mean that it will work for you. It is interesting that, even among the small group of downshifters who are participating in this book, are both Harriet who wanted to escape into teaching (see opposite) and Patrick who had to quit education in part because of the stress (see Chapter 7). It seems one man's (or woman's) meat is another's poison.

Changing career can also put an enormous strain on you financially if it involves a period of retraining. It may be impossible to move into your chosen new career without acquiring new qualifications – for example, if you need a Post-Graduate Certificate of Education (PGCE) or a teaching English as a foreign language (TEFL) qualification in order to become a teacher. You need to plan

Harriet's story

Harriet worked for a long time as a civil servant doing finance work with the Ministry of Defence. The nine-to-five routine and stress of the job made her intensely miserable and started to affect the whole of her life, including the relationships with her husband and daughter. *'I didn't feel I was doing anything I enjoyed or anything where I was valued.'*

After battling with the decision for two years, Harriet finally decided to make the break and leave. Her intention was to take a year out and then apply to do a post-graduate certificate of education so she could teach primary school children. *'After working for about nine months doing temp jobs I attended my PGCE interview – and then learnt I had not been successful ... I didn't know what to do. I hadn't even thought about what I would do if I didn't get on to the course.'*

'I decided that a career change wasn't going to happen, so I found a permanent job doing more finance work. I lasted about three months and I hated it. The job was rubbish, the company hopeless and I hated doing the work. I felt very frustrated with the monotonous nature of the work. I wanted to do a job that I felt was more valuable in terms of doing something useful. My work was making my life and my husband's and daughter's lives so miserable. I had to leave. No job was worth being so unhappy, so I just handed in my notice and left.'

Harriet had no other work lined up, so went back to temping but this time in schools and colleges. In a couple of days, she was offered a part-time, temporary job as a learning support assistant. Two months later, she was taken on permanently. *'I now work 26 hours a week and love it. I am doing a sign language course and an Open University course and am the happiest I have ever been ... It's hard to explain just how good it has been. I am still in the process of changing careers – I hope to do a PGCE part-time and teach in further education colleges.'*

Both Harriet's work and family life have improved. *'I spend time doing my courses as well as doing things around the house and more time doing things for and with my family. I have finally achieved exactly the life/work balance I was hoping for ... I am so pleased I left finance work, but only sorry it took me so long to make the decision.'*

how you will cope financially during your training or whether there are alternative approaches, such as combining part-time study with part-time work (see Chapter 5) which would be financially more feasible even if it means you have to take longer achieving your downshift. If a new qualification is desirable but not essential, it might be possible to study part-time or through day release while simultaneously starting to work in your chosen new career at a lower level than you ultimately hope to achieve.

Leaving a job

Your legal rights when leaving voluntarily

Your motives for choosing voluntarily to switch to another job or career may be negative, positive or a mixture of the two. Negative reasons centre on dissatisfaction with your current job – maybe it is too stressful, the hours too long, or the work no longer stimulates you. Positive reasons for making a change include a desire to try out some other specific career that you have already identified as a goal.

If you are leaving a job voluntarily, there are generally no legal rights or duties to consider beyond the need to give adequate notice. However, in some limited circumstances where you are leaving for negative reasons, even if you seem to be leaving voluntarily, the law might give you rights to claim compensation if your reason for leaving was treatment that amounted to constructive dismissal – see opposite.

You will need to give your employer notice. By law, the minimum notice you must give is one week, assuming you have been employed continuously for at least a month. Your contract might specify a longer period.

While you are reaching a decision about whether to leave, you might need to investigate matters such as the amount of pension you might get if you take early retirement or the pension rights you can transfer. Until you are certain that you will be leaving, you might want to be discreet about making enquiries since, once your employer suspects you might be leaving, you are less likely to be considered for any career development measures, such as training or promotion. This could hold you back if you change your mind and decide not to leave after all.

Your legal rights if you are dismissed

Not all job or career switches, of course, are voluntary. For example, being dismissed can trigger a downshift. At the time, a forced downshift might seem a disaster, but in the longer run could turn out to be beneficial if it takes you down a path which you had not quite plucked up the courage to initiate yourself. Your employer must have sound reasons for dismissing you and follow set procedures, otherwise you might have a claim for unfair dismissal – see *Further information* on page 70.

If you choose to leave but feel you were forced to quit, you might have a case to claim compensation for constructive dismissal. Constructive dismissal is a type of unfair dismissal and describes the situation where your employer breaks your contract of employment in some fundamental way – for example, imposing a change in the nature or your work – that is so intolerable you feel forced to resign. You must have worked for the employer continuously for at least a year to be eligible to bring an unfair dismissal claim.

Your contract of employment

When you take up a job, you enter into a contract with your employer which places obligations on you both. This is the case even if your contract is just oral and not written down. However, with any job lasting longer than a month, you do have the right to a written statement setting out the main terms and conditions of your job, such as the hours you will work, how much holiday you get, your right to sick pay, and so on. There may be other terms which are not spelt out in writing but are customary or implied.

Stress in the workplace

Your downshift may be triggered by what you feel is the unacceptable stress of your job. You would not be alone – claims for incapacity benefit (a main state benefit for people of working age who cannot work because of illness) due to mental disorders are on the increase. But a recent court case suggests you have only limited rights to claim against your employer for work-related stress.

Leon Barber was employed by Somerset County Council working as both a maths teacher and maths co-ordinator in a secondary school. His dual role and lack of deputies meant he regularly worked 61 to 70 hours a week and his health suffered as a result. In May 1996 he was signed off sick for three weeks due to depression. Mr Barber complained to the school about his workload, but nothing was done. Returning to work after the summer break, the stress continued and in November 1996 Mr Barber became so ill that he has not worked since.

Mr Barber brought a case against his employer which initially he won, lost on appeal and then won again in the House of Lords. The proceedings established some principles to be applied in cases of stress at work. An employer is entitled to assume that employees can withstand the normal pressures of a job. But, if an employer knows or should know that an individual employee is vulnerable to stress or has been warned that mental damage might occur, then the employer has a duty to take reasonable steps to protect the worker from harm. In Mr Barber's case, the bout of depression in May 1996 should have alerted the employer to his vulnerability. In addition, Mr Barber had told the senior managers at the school that he was having problems. Reasonable steps an employer could take would probably include giving all employees access to a confidential counselling service.

Your legal rights if you are made redundant

If your job disappears – for example, your employer is slimming down the workforce or no longer requires people to do your particular type of work – you may be made redundant.

If 20 or more employees are to be made redundant within a 90-day period, your employer must consult with your union or, if there is no union, other staff representative body. If there is no such body, representatives may be appointed specifically for this consultation. In rare situations where there is no union or other staff representation at all, the employer must deal with you direct.

Your employer must normally give you personally at least the notice required by law (see overleaf) or set out in your contract. But, with your employer's agreement, you can leave early without jeopardising your rights to redundancy pay.

By law, if you are being made redundant, your employer must give you reasonable time off to look for another job or arrange training. This is paid time off but the minimum amount of pay is worked out according to a formula and may be less than your normal rate.

The consultation process is typically used to examine whether jobs can be saved, how the people to be made redundant are to be selected, the impact on pensions, and importantly the financial side of the redundancy package. As part of the package, you might be offered access to a financial adviser.

Redundancy pay can be an important element helping you to finance a downshift, though the statutory amount your employer must pay you by law (see Table 4.1) is relatively small. In the year from 1 February 2004, the maximum statutory payout would be $20 \times £270 \times 1.5 = £8,100$. But, particularly where your employer is trying to encourage people to step forward for voluntary redundancy, the package on offer could be much larger.

The statutory redundancy payments shown in the Table 4.1 may be reduced if you are taking early retirement or will within 90 weeks after becoming redundant start to receive a pension from an occupational scheme run by your employer. There are limits on the amount of redundancy pay that can be replaced in this way.

If you are aged 64, your redundancy pay is reduced by one-twelfth for each month since your sixty-fourth birthday. From age 65 onwards, you are not entitled to any statutory redundancy pay at all.

Table 4.1 How much statutory redundancy pay?

For each year of continuous service between the ages	You are entitled to this much statutory redundancy pay	Limit on pay	Limit on years of service
Under 18	Nothing	Not applicable	Not applicable
18–21 22–40 41–63 64	½ week's pay 1 week's pay 1½ week's pay 1½ week's pay but reduced by one-twelfth for each month you are over age 64	The pay on which this is based is capped at £270 a week from 1 February 2004	The maximum number of years' continuous service on which this is based is 20
65 and over	Nothing	Not applicable	Not applicable

Legal rights on changing jobs within the same firm

In general terms, neither you nor your employer can alter the terms of your job without the consent of the other. So, normally, if you see another job within your firm that you would like to switch to, you have the normal rights of any jobseeker applying to fill a vacancy – see page 62. If there are no specific vacancies, you could negotiate with your employer to switch to other work, but your employer does not have to agree.

Similarly, your employer cannot normally just transfer you to other work, unless it is an explicit term of your contract that you can be required to do different types of work or move to a different location. If that's not the case and your employer wants you to shift to another job within the firm, he or she must negotiate with you.

You might accept or simply go along with the change without voicing any complaint, in which case you will be deemed to have accepted. Alternatively, you have the right to refuse, but your employer can then legally end your employment. All normal termination rights apply, so for example you must be given proper notice (or pay in lieu of notice). Your contract of employment may specify a longer notice period but by law you must be given at least the minimum notice period you must be given by law:

- one week's notice if you have been with the employer at least a month but less than two years
- two weeks' notice if you have been with the employer at least two years plus one additional week for each year up to a maximum of 12 weeks' notice.

If your existing job is ceasing to exist, you may be entitled to redundancy rights – see page 59.

If your employer simply imposes a change of job on you without seeking your consent, your employer has broken the contract and you can claim damages if you lose financially as a result. You can choose whether to make a claim through the courts or an employment tribunal. A tribunal is usually quicker and cheaper. You may be able to make such a claim even if you resigned if you were a victim of constructive unfair dismissal (see page 57).

Starting your new job or career

Finding a new job or career

You may already be clear about the new job or career you want to switch to. Try to gather as much information as you can about it. For example, contact relevant professional and trade bodies for information. If you can, talk to people already working in that field. Is there any chance of gaining some work experience in the area, for example, by taking related part-time work or, say, if you want to teach, could you help as a classroom assistant?

If you will first have to study or train, seek out appropriate courses. Your local library should have directories of courses in its reference section. Alternatively use the Internet. The websites of LearnDirect★, the Universities and Colleges Admission Service (UCAS)★ and Higher Education & Research Opportunities in the UK (HERO)★ have useful search features to help you narrow down your choice. Once you have a shortlist, visit the websites of the colleges, universities or other bodies offering the courses concerned for more information. If you want to study from home, check out courses with the Open University (OU)★. If you do not have access to the Internet at home or work, bear in mind that most public libraries, community colleges and adult learning centres now have computers you can use very cheaply or free of charge.

Educational institutions generally have their own careers centres and should also be able to give you advice about the work the courses can lead on to.

If you are unsure about what career or job to go for, consider getting help from a careers service*. You pay a fee but these firms can help you analyse what you want, identify suitable careers and help you prepare a CV.

Local employment agencies* have details of jobs in your area, permanent, part-time and temporary. Other places to look are newspapers and the Internet. If you are unemployed – for example, following redundancy, your local Jobcentre Plus* offers advice on finding work as well as advertising jobs and dealing with claims for state benefits for which you may be eligible (see Chapter 11).

Your legal rights applying for a job

By law, employers must not discriminate on the grounds of sex, marital status, disability, race, sexual orientation or religious or similar beliefs. This applies to job advertisements and recruitment processes as well as the workplace once you have started a job.

If you feel you have been a victim of discrimination on any of the above grounds, you can take a complaint to an employment tribunal.

People who are changing jobs or career, might already have a few years behind them and, at present, age could be a disadvantage in getting a new job. According to a survey for the Chartered Institute of Personnel Development, the only age group that is unlikely to be deemed either too young or too old for a job is 35- to 40-year-olds. However, from October 2006, age discrimination is to be outlawed. Changing the law is one thing; changing employer's attitudes may take longer. But, in time, the new legislation should make it easier for more mature workers to change jobs and careers.

Bear in mind that you should not be paid less than the national minimum wage, which is £4.85 an hour before tax from 1 October 2004 for people aged 22 and over.

Financial aspects of changing jobs or career

Lump sums on leaving a job

You may well receive a lump sum when you leave your old job, especially if you have been made redundant or taken early retirement.

Any lump sum may in fact be made up of several different amounts paid to you for different purposes. How these sums are taxed varies depending on their purpose.

Any amount that is paid in accordance with your contract or that you could expect as a result of your contract is taxable in the same way as any other pay. For example, this includes:

- any salary due to you
- holiday pay
- pay in lieu of notice, unless it was neither due under the terms of your contract nor customary for your employer to make such payments
- any bonus in recognition of the work you have done
- any amount you receive in return for a 'restrictive covenant', for example an agreement that you will not go into competition with the employer.

Some payments are completely tax-free and these include:

- a lump sum from an occupational pension scheme
- a payment you receive because of an accident at work.

Most other payments are tax-free up to the first £30,000. If the total of such payments is more than £30,000, the rest counts as taxable income, usually in the year you receive the payment. These amounts count towards the £30,000 limit:

- statutory redundancy pay
- any other redundancy pay
- pay in lieu of notice that is not taxed as described above
- any other amounts that were not due under the terms of your contract or customary or expected in your job.

Where the payments are taxable, your employer will usually have deducted any tax and National Insurance through PAYE before making the payments to you. If you have received amounts that have not been taxed but on which tax is due, you will need to declare them and pay tax through the self-assessment system. See Chapter 12 for details.

Impact on your income

If you are switching to lower-paid work, you will have to adapt to living on a smaller income, in which case see Chapter 9 for ideas to help you budget soundly.

You may need to retrain to take up your new career, in which case you could face a period without any income coming in. Lump sums from leaving your old job might help to tide you over. You might – like John and Jenny (see page 70) – release money by selling your home and buying somewhere cheaper, or perhaps have other assets you could sell or savings you could use.

Another option is to borrow, though you should take care to plan how you will repay your loans. If your retraining involves going to university, you might be eligible for a student loan and/or other help – see page 66.

Impact on your spending

It is impossible to generalise about how your spending might change if you switch job or career. There certainly could be savings if, say, you have been commuting to work but will no longer have to do so after the downshift. But, in general terms, since you are continuing to work, all the normal work-related expenses might continue. Use the calculator in Chapter 9 to help you consider what impact your own particular job or career switch might have.

The one aspect of this type of downshift that will have a major, albeit temporary, impact on your spending is if you have to retrain in order to take up your new job or career. During a sustained period of study or training, you might have a much reduced income and need to pull on your spending horns. You may also have additional spending needs, for example, on tuition fees, books, a computer, and so on. If you have to live away from home to attend your course, you'll usually have to pay rent. Many mature students live at home while studying, but the savings on rent might be outweighed by higher travelling costs unless your home is close to college or you are prepared to move house in order to be closer.

Surveys of younger students have also found that the savings from living at home while studying tend also to be reduced because home-based students often spend more on books and computing than students who are campus-based. Again Chapter 9 will help you think about how your spending will change during this period of your downshift.

Impact on your pension

A brief outline is given here of how your pension might be affected if you change your job or career. For more detail about how different types of pension scheme work and why they might be affected, see Chapter 12.

State pension

If you move straight from one job to another, there will be no loss of state basic pension unless your new job is very low-paid (less than £79 a week in 2004–5).

Your state additional pension may be affected if you start to be or cease to be 'contracted out', though taking any occupational pension together with state pension, you may not be particularly better or worse off.

If you take time out to study, this will appear as a gap in your National Insurance contributions record and might reduce your eventual basic pension. Consider whether it would be worth making Class 3 contributions to prevent this. You will not be building up state additional pension while studying and there is nothing you can do about that.

Occupational pension

If you belonged to an occupational pension scheme through your old job but you had been a member for less than two years, you will usually be offered a refund of your own (but not your employer's) contributions. You might welcome the lump sum, but you will be back to square one as far as pension savings for the last two years are concerned, so you might want to consider topping up your pension savings.

If you have been in the scheme for two years or more, you are entitled to a 'preserved pension'. You can either leave this to build up in the scheme or transfer your pension rights to a new scheme –

which at best is not an easy decision. Get a transfer statement from the old scheme to find out the amount of money you can transfer to a new scheme. Get a quote from the new scheme, saying how much pension you might get by retirement if you paid in the transfer value. Where a large sum is involved, consider getting professional advice (see *Further information*, page 70).

If your new employer offers an occupational pension scheme, it will often be the best way to save for retirement.

Personal pensions

You do not have to make changes to any personal pension just because you change job or career. If income will be tight – for example, because you become a student – you might want to suspend your contributions for a while. This will, of course, reduce your eventual pension.

Before suspending contributions, check whether there are any penalties for doing this. There will not be in the case of a stakeholder pension.

Financial help if you are a mature student

In general terms, if you are UK resident, you can qualify for help from the state with the costs of going to university. However, if you took a degree in the past with the help of public funding, you are unlikely to qualify for further funding now – but there are exceptions, so check your eligibility with the local education authority (LEA)* for the area in which you live.

There is also an age limit on access to student loans. Many types of help are means-tested, so you will qualify only if your income is low.

Here is a brief summary of the types of financial help you might be able to get if you live in England or Wales. Arrangements are slightly different in Scotland and Northern Ireland. See *Further information* on page 70 for how to find out more.

Fees

In the academic years 2004–5, if your household income is less than £21,475, the state will pick up the full tab for your tuition fees. This help tapers away to nothing for incomes of £31,973 or more, but the most you'll have to pay is £1,150 for the year. Tuition fees have to be paid up-front at the start of each academic year. The income assessment is based on your own income and that of your spouse or partner if you have one, although some types of income are ignored.

The same system applies to students starting in the 2005–6 academic year. The maximum fees contribution is increased each year in line with inflation, so will be a little more than £1,150 in 2005–6.

The system is due to change for students (other than those who have taken a gap year in 2005–6) starting courses in autumn 2006 or later. At the time of writing, the required legislation is still making its way through Parliament, but assuming it goes through largely unchanged, the system will be as follows. Universities will be able to charge different fees up to a maximum of £3,000 a year. The amount you pay will vary depending on both the university and the course you choose. You will no longer have to pay the fees up-front. Instead you may be able to take out a student loan (see below) to cover the fees and then repay this gradually once your course is over and you are working.

If your household income is low, you might qualify for a higher education grant (see below) and/or a bursary from your university to help you cope with the cost of fees.

Student loan

If you are under age 50 at the start of your course, you are eligible to apply for a student loan. If you are aged 50 to 54, you might be able to apply but only if you can show that you plan to return to work after your course.

Currently student loans are intended to help you meet your living costs. From autumn 2006, it is expected that you will also be able to take out loans to pay your tuition fees (see above). In 2004–5, the maximum student loan is £5,050 if you are studying in London and £4,095 if you are studying elsewhere.

A quarter of the loan to meet living costs is means-tested so you get it only if your household income is low enough. The means-tested part is reduced for higher incomes and not available at all if your income is above a certain level. Table 4.2 shows the level of income at which you do not qualify for this part of the loan at all and the maximum you'll have to pay yourself assuming you make up the amount out of your own resources. The remaining three-quarters of the student loan to cover living costs is available whatever your income.

Student loans are a cheap way to borrow compared with other types of loan. You do not pay interest as such. Instead the outstanding loan is increased each year in line with inflation. You do not start to repay the loan until after your course has ended. You then make repayments only if your income is above a given level (£10,000 a year, due to rise to £15,000 a year from April 2005). Your repayments are set at 9 per cent of your income above that threshold. For example, if you earned £20,000 in 2005–6, you would repay 9% × (£20,000 – £15,000) = £450. You can pay off more if you like.

No more repayments are required once you reach age 65, you become permanently disabled or you die.

Table 4.2 Maximum you must pay towards tuition fees and living costs in 2004–5

	Full year of study		Final year of study	
	If your household income is at least this much	You are expected to pay this much	If your household income is at least this much	You are expected to pay this much
Tuition fees only	£31,973	£1,150	£31,973	£1,150
Tuition fees plus means-tested student loan: London rate	£43,943	£2,410	£42,375	£2,245
Tuition fees plus means-tested student loan: elsewhere rate	£41,710	£2,175	£40,428	£2,040

Source: Department for Education and Skills

Higher education grant

This is a means-tested, non-repayable grant available whatever your age. If your household income is £15,200 or less in 2004–5 you can get the full amount. The sum is reduced for higher incomes and no grant is available if your income is £21,185 or above.

Students with children

If you are a parent, there are various means-tested grants that you might be able to claim to help you with, for example, childcare costs. See *Further information*, page 70.

You might also qualify for child tax credit – see Chapter 11.

Access to Learning Fund

Your college can make grants in cases of hardship to meet particular costs or to help you in an emergency.

Training to be a teacher

The government is keen to encourage more people to take up teaching, particularly in subjects where there is a particular shortage, so there are various incentives available.

If you are not already a teacher and you take a post-graduate teaching course (such as a Post Graduate Certificate of Education), your fees will be paid in full. You might also qualify for a £6,000 training bursary.

If you are training either at undergraduate or post-graduate level to become a secondary teacher in a shortage subject, you might qualify for a means-tested bursary of up to £7,500.

Health-related studies

Bursaries are available from the National Health Service for people studying health professional courses (such as midwifery, physiotherapy and speech therapy), medicine or dentistry.

Medical and dental students might also qualify for help with the costs of travelling to the site of their clinical training.

Social work students

Bursaries are available if you are studying for a degree or diploma in social work.

Part-time students

Provided your course is equivalent to at least half of a full-time course, you might qualify for up to £575 a year towards fees and up to £250 a year to help with the cost of books, travel, and so on.

Career development loan

If you do not qualify for a student loan, bursary of other state help, you might nevertheless be able to get a career development loan. This is a commercial loan available from participating banks under a scheme run jointly with the Department for Education and Skills (DFES). While you are on your course and for one month afterwards, the DFES pays the interest and you make no repayments. After that, you are charged interest and must make repayments.

These loans are available for up to two years to fund education or vocational training and a further year if the course involves practical work experience. You can borrow between £300 and £8,000.

John and Jenny's story

'Both me and my wife have given up the rat race and quit the day jobs – her as a computer programmer, me as an engineer/manager – and gone back to college. Our fortieth birthdays were approaching and we decided to look for a career change as we were not getting any younger. The day jobs were no longer challenging and the ageism and qualifications culture were both preventing serious advancement.'

Initially, John and Jenny were not sure what they would do. Their first option – emigration, possibly continuing to work in their current fields – was ruled out because they were considered too old unless they had specific jobs to go to. But they had long been keen on diving and devoted many holidays abroad to this hobby. They had been especially stimulated by dives with a marine biologist, so they decided to look further into new careers as marine biologists and coastal engineers.

They found an ideal university course, involving plenty of practical as well as theoretical work. *'So far we are doing OK and are halfway through the three-year course already. The course has provided opportunities to undertake field trips to Scotland, and a marine reserve off the South American coast where we undertook research for the Honduran government. The research was coupled with managing a park and the marine fauna and flora within it, so while this was volunteer work, it has already started to fulfil our objectives of getting to warm, sunny places and doing worthwhile work.'*

John and Jenny are funding their training mainly through the sale of their home in the south of England. They moved to Blackpool where they are studying. Because house prices are cheaper, they

---

were able to buy a larger house and still fund their downshift. The larger house gives them scope to take in lodgers if they need extra money, though so far they have not had to do that. John has also been taken on as a part-time lab technician at the college. *'This work is associated with the course anyway, so no real stress there and it is some income. My wife's free-time increase has allowed her to restart her home shopping distributorship at hours to suit us so there is income there as well.'*

How do John and Jenny sum up their downshift? *'So far, very good. Less stress, more free time, no middle of the night call outs, much better nightlife, new friends, milder climate (it's less extreme by the sea), less work than the old job, more choice in what is done and when – better quality of life.'*

Further information

For more about your rights in connection with your job, see the free booklets listed below.

Table 4.3 Free information about your rights at work

Reference code	Title	Available from
PL810	Contracts of employment	Department of Trade and Industry*
PL707	Rights to notice and reasons for dismissal	
PL712	Unfairly dismissed?	
PL808	Redundancy entitlement – statutory rights	
	Protection against discrimination at work on grounds of religion of belief	
	Protection against discrimination at work on grounds of sexual orientation	
	Code of practice – sex discrimination	Equal Opportunities Commission*
	The duty to promote race equality: code of practice and guidance	Commission for Racial Equality*
	Code of practice on employment	Disability Rights Commission*
IR204	Lump sums and compensation payments	Inland Revenue*

If you need professional help with a decision about transferring a pension, contact an independent financial adviser (IFA)★ or, if a large sum is involved, a consulting actuary★.

To find out more about financial help for students, see *Financial support for higher education students*, available from the Department for Education and Skills (DfES)★ or the local education authority (LEA)★ for the area in which you live. If you have children, see also *Childcare grants and other support for student parents in higher education* from the same sources.

To find out about the system in Scotland, contact the Student Awards Agency for Scotland (SAAS)★. For Northern Ireland, contact the Student Support Branch of the Department for Employment and Learning Northern Ireland★.

To find out about the tax credits, contact the Inland Revenue★.

For details of the incentives available to people training as teachers, contact the Teaching Information Line★.

If you are considering a medical or dental course, get *Financial help for healthcare students* from the Department of Health★ or *Financial help for healthcare students in Wales* from NHS Wales Student Awards Unit★.

The General Social Care Council★ can provide information about financial help for social work students.

Career development loans are available from the following banks: Barclays, Co-operative Bank and Royal Bank of Scotland. Application forms are available from branches of these banks and also from Jobcentre Plus★ offices or the government's Lifelong Learning★ website.

Chapter 5

Working part-time or job-sharing

Maybe you like your current job but just wish there was less of it. Or you might be looking for a new job but with limited hours. The two main courses open to you are to work part-time or to job-share.

Do not make the mistake of thinking job-sharing is the same as merely working part-time. Ordinary part-time work involves doing a job which is fully self-contained within the specified hours. Job-sharing means spreading a full-time job across two people. It involves additional skills and responsibilities because you need to work closely and communicate effectively with your job-share partner. The two halves of the job will not necessarily be identical, and each half-job will not necessarily reflect all aspects of the full-time job.

Part-time work, including job-sharing, can be appealing for many reasons. A common motive is to combine work and parenting, particularly where a part-time job can be fitted in during school hours. Part-time work can also be ideal if you are older and want to ease back on work in the run up to full retirement, in which case you might start to draw some pension to supplement your earnings. At younger ages, you might choose part-time work simply to have more time for your own interests. Another motive is to allow time to start up your own business while using the earnings from part-time work to carry you through the first few years of your start-up – although this might involve doing more rather than less work for now, it could be a stepping stone to a downshifted life running your own business (see Chapter 7).

The main drawback to working shorter hours is lower pay. Unless yours is a very high-paid line of work, you may need other resources to support you – for example, a partner who is also earning, a pension from early retirement, income from investments, and so on.

However, the loss of income may be less than you expected once savings in tax, National Insurance and other areas are taken into account (see page 85).

A further possible drawback is that, depending on the culture and attitudes in your workplace and the nature of your work, you might also find that working part-time or job-sharing limits your prospects for career advancement.

Lesley's story

After the birth of her first child in 1990, Lesley decided to return to work but on a part-time basis so that she could juggle her hours to fit the family.

'I looked at the financial implications of having a full-time job and using a childminder, but I felt the amount of money left at the end of the month did not make it worth leaving my child to be brought up by a stranger. The job I did at the time involved being a help-desk adviser, doing security back-ups and running month-end accounts. I felt it could not be done to 100 per cent of my abilities working part-time or job-sharing.'

So Lesley switched to a different job and now works in accounts. Initially she worked evenings and weekends while her husband was home to take over the childcare. Now, Lesley has three children aged 13, 11 and 8. *'Working part-time means I can juggle my hours. In the school holiday, I work full days and, in term-time, I work five hours a day between 9.30am and 2.30pm. My husband and I take time off in the school holidays separately to cover most of the holiday time.*

'I would not want promotion or extra hours as I have a balanced life. I have always worked hours which fit around school life. This has meant my children have never been to a childminder. I feel it is important for them and for me to be home when they come in from school and to have my full attention for help and support with homework, etc.'

The only drawback Lesley has found is the attitude of some employers towards part-timers: *'When you work part-time, people don't see you as committed to work as much as full-timers.'* This makes her reluctant to take time off even when sick and means she feels less secure in her job than if she worked full-time.

Who currently works reduced hours?

Out of some 28.3 million people in work in the UK, just over a quarter (7.4 million) work part-time – see Chart 5.1. The proportion is much higher among women than men, with 44 per cent of women working part-time compared with just 11 per cent of men. The vast majority of part-timers say they work part-time because they do not want a full-time job, not because of any difficulty finding full-time work or other circumstances.

Job-sharing is a special type of part-time working where two people split a full-time post between them. Around 1 per cent of the workforce currently job-shares (almost double the number compared with ten years ago). Again, many more women than men job-share (179,000 women compared with 19,000 men in 2002).

Term-time working

Like Lesley (see opposite), many women opt for part-time work in order to fit around their parental commitments. Another option offered by some employers is term-time working. Under this arrangement, you work full-time during school terms and take unpaid leave during the holidays, though your pay may be spread evenly throughout the year. The availability of this option often depends on the employer being able to employ, say, students during the holiday period.

Chart 5.1 Part-time working in the UK

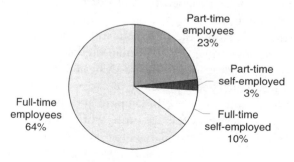

Source: Labour Force Survey, January–March 2004

Your right to contain the hours you work

Your desire to work shorter hours might not be as dramatic as shifting to part-time work. You might simply want to work 'normal' hours and, in theory, you do have this right. Under European law, you cannot be forced to work long hours. In particular, you have the right to:

- a maximum working week of 48 hours on average, including overtime
- a minimum rest period of 11 consecutive hours each day
- no more than eight hours of night work on average in a 24-hour period
- a rest break if your working day is longer than six hours
- at least one day a week free of work
- four weeks' paid holiday a year.

However, when it comes to the hours you work each week, in the UK there is an 'opt-out' from the main rules. The opt-out means that you can be required to work more than 48 hours a week if, in advance, you have agreed in writing to do so. Your agreement should be voluntary and the law specifically states that you should neither be pressured into signing up for longer hours nor suffer any disadvantage if you decide not to.

That's the theory. In practice, some employers put the opt-out statement in the contract you must sign on taking up a job. As the European authorities have pointed out, this is at odds with the legal requirements, since you hardly have a free choice if the opt-out is presented as a condition of employment. In total, nearly a fifth of UK employees have signed the opt-out either as part of their contract or separately.

At the time of writing, the European authorities were reviewing this area of the law and had yet to decide whether the UK would be allowed to keep the opt-out in future. A heated debate was taking place with arguments being put both for and against the status quo.

Those in favour of the UK keeping its opt-out claim that workers themselves want the option to work long hours, in particular to earn overtime pay. They also say the opt-out is necessary if businesses are to have the flexibility to meet surges in demand. They point out that this is a precautionary measure and, in practice, in four-fifths of firms where employees have signed the opt-out, there is in fact no record of long hours being worked on a sustained basis. A survey for the government found that long hours are most likely among senior managers and manual workers, particularly in the transport and communication sectors of the economy. Long hours are more often found in small businesses than larger firms.

Those lobbying for the opt-out to be abolished point out that UK employees have the longest working hours in Europe and the UK is the only European Union country where average working hours have risen rather than fallen over the last ten years. They argue that UK workers have little choice but to work these long hours which cause stress, low morale and damage to family life.

The upshot is that, under the current rules, you have the legal right to limit your working week to no more than an average 48 hours. You might find it hard to exercise this right, but it could be worth sticking to your legal guns if you feel reducing the hours you work is important enough.

Your right to work part-time

A job you do already

Since April 2003, some parents have the right to request flexible working (see below). But, in other circumstances, you generally do not have any right to switch from full-time to part-time or flexible working (unless unusually your contract says so).

However, many employers do offer the option of part-time working, flexi-time and/or job-sharing, so it is worth checking whether your employer has a specific policy on this. Even if there is no policy, try asking your employer to consider such a request. To strengthen your case, think through as far as possible the implications for your employer and colleagues and work out how any problems might be overcome.

Parental right to flexible working
If you are already in a job and you are a parent of a child under the age of six, or under 18 if the child has a disability, you have the right to ask your employer to consider a request to let you work flexibly.

To be eligible, you must have worked for your employer for at least six months and you must not have made a similar request within the last year.

Flexible working could take many forms. For example, it could mean working part-time, job-sharing, working full-time but flexing your hours, compressed hours (working more hours per day but on fewer days per week), working from home part of the time, and so on.

The onus is on you to state what flexibility you want. It would be worth taking some time to prepare a well-thought-out plan and to include alternatives – for example, if ideally you would prefer a job-share, state other options you would be happy with if job-sharing does not prove possible. You should make your request in writing. (The Department of Trade and Industry (DTI)* produces a form

---

A parent's right to request flexible working: application checklist

An application under the right must:

- be in writing (whether on paper, email or fax)
- state the application is being made under the statutory right to request a flexible working pattern
- confirm the employee has responsibility for the upbringing of the child and is either: the mother, father, adopter, guardian or foster parent; or, married to or the partner of the child's mother, father, adopter, guardian or foster parent
- explain what effect, if any, the employee thinks the proposed change would have on the employer and how, in their opinion, any such effect might be dealt with
- specify the flexible working pattern applied for
- state the date on which it is proposed the change should become effective
- state whether a previous application has been made to the employer and if so, when it was made
- be dated.

Source: Department of Trade and Industry

FW(A) *Flexible working application form* which you might find helpful but you do not have to use it.) The checklist opposite, produced by the DTI, sets out the information you should include in your request.

Your employer has a duty to consider the request seriously and must meet with you to discuss it, but does not have to agree to it. However, your employer must give sound business reasons for refusal, for example, because it would be too costly to implement, it would affect quality or performance, or it would be impossible to reorganise the work given existing staff. Your employer must notify you in writing whether your request has been granted or refused. You have the right to appeal against the decision and, if you think consent has been unreasonably withheld, you can take your case to an employment tribunal. The written notice from your employer must set out the appeals procedure.

A new job for which you are applying

Clearly, if you are seeking part-time work, there is little point applying for full-time posts – stick to those jobs which are advertised as part-time.

The position is more tricky when it comes to job-sharing. Although many employers say they consider job-shares, very few jobs are advertised as being available on this basis. The onus is normally on you to find out whether the firm advertising the full-time post would consider offering it on a job-share basis. You can approach this in several ways:

- ask the prospective employer during the selection process whether they would consider a job-share. The advantage of raising the issue at this stage is that the employer can then ask other applicants if they would be interested in job-sharing which increases the chance of a job-share partner being found. The disadvantage is that the employer might not like the idea of job-sharing and may think you would not be committed to the job as a full-time post.
- wait until you are offered the full-time post and then suggest a job-share. By this time it might be too late to ask other applicants if they would be interested in sharing the job, so even if your employer is sympathetic to the idea, it might be impossible

to put it into practice straight away. In the meantime, you will be working full-time.

- wait until you are established in the job and then request a change. Again it may be tricky to find a potential job-share partner and you could end up working on a full-time basis for much longer than you would ideally like.

In teaching, where job-sharing is no longer quite so novel, some local education authorities – for example, Essex County Council – have started a register of people interested in job-sharing. This is useful because you can search for a potential job-share partner *before* applying for jobs. You and your partner can then jointly apply to fill advertised full-time posts. Since this removes a major obstacle to job-sharing (the lack of a partner), it should increase your chances of getting the job you want on the basis you want.

If you have a way of identifying other people working in your field – for example, through membership of a professional body or trade union – consider advertising for a potential job-share partner before starting to job hunt.

Compressed hours

Some employers offer a range of different options for employees who are seeking a more flexible approach to work. An alternative to going part-time might be to work 'compressed hours'. This involves, say, working a given number of hours per fortnight. Typically, workers in a department might organise between themselves who will cover which hours and tend to opt for longish shifts which results in more days per fortnight completely clear of work. The extra days off might then be, for example, spent with family or used for studying. If you are interested in this way of working, ask your employer if there is already a compressed hours policy at your workplace and, if not, whether this is an option that could be introduced.

Practical aspects of working part-time

The law protects part-time workers, stating that they must not be treated less favourably than equivalent full-time workers. Of course, that does not mean that you should get exactly the same pay, holidays, and so on – these will be scaled down in line with the hours you work. So, for example, if you work half the number of hours, you can expect half the pay and half the holiday.

However, apart from scaling back your pay and benefits pro rata, you can by law expect to be treated the same as other employees. This protection applies from the first day you start your job. It applies to more or less any term or condition of your job, including pay, benefits, access to a pension scheme at work, holidays, training, sick pay, parental leave, inclusion in career break schemes, and so on.

The tricky part in bringing any claim for less favourable treatment may be identifying an equivalent full-time worker against whom to compare yourself. If you have recently switched from full-time to part-time work, you might be able to use yourself as a comparison.

Note that access to state benefits handled by your employer, such as statutory sick pay and statutory maternity pay, depend on your earning at least the lower earnings limit (£79 a week in 2004–5). This limit is the same for all employees, even part-timers – it is not scaled down. So, if your part-time pay is less than the limit, your employer will not be able to give you these payments. You may be eligible for other state benefits instead (see Chapter 11).

Women who work part-time might also have some protection under the laws which ban sex discrimination at work. This could be the case if, for example, your workplace gives particular benefits to full-timers – say, private medical insurance or a bonus scheme – that it denies part-timers, and the majority of the part-timers are women. This could count as indirect sex discrimination.

If you believe you are being treated unfairly because of your part-time status (or sex), first write to your employer. If you do not get a satisfactory response, you can take your case to an employment tribunal.

Practical aspects of job-sharing

Your employer might have an existing policy on job-sharing – according to a survey in 1999 for the Institute of Personnel and Development (now the Chartered Institute for Personnel and Development), 57 per cent of its members claimed that job-sharing was available as an option for employees.

How job-sharing works

Typically two people take on a job which traditionally has been a single post. The job-share can work in various ways. For example, the job-share partners might do the same job merely covering different hours. Alternatively, they might do different parts of the job or take on different projects.

The reduction in hours can also be tackled in different ways, for example the partners might work:

- on different days during the week,
- either mornings or afternoons, or
- alternate weeks.

Pay and benefits are split between the two of you. There are no hard and fast rules for how this is done and it will depend what's in the remuneration package. For example, if the job when full-time comes with a company car, perhaps each of you might be offered a car allowance up to half the value of the normal company car. If you work different days in the week, there will need to be some adjustment to allocate bank holidays since many of these occur on Mondays.

From your employer's point of view, the job-share may work out more expensive than the single full-time post it replaces because, for example, the employer will have double the training bill, double the line management responsibilities, time will be lost in communication and handovers between the partners, and so on. However, there could be some saving on employer's National Insurance contributions and indirect savings if absenteeism is lower.

Depending on the nature of the job, the employer can also benefit if the job-share results in a bigger flow of ideas ('two heads are better than one'), the partners covering for each other, partners putting in more than their strictly contractual hours, two staff instead of one to take on extra tasks (which might be especially important in, say, a school where staff often volunteer to run clubs and other extra-curricular activities). When selling the idea of a job-share to your employer, it would be worth drawing attention to any such potential benefits.

Jobs most suited to job-sharing

To date, job-sharing has been most common with largely clerical and administrative jobs, but there is some indication that it is becoming available for managerial and professional jobs too. Schools, universities, local government and the National Health Service are areas where job-sharing is most common.

In general terms, job-sharing may be easiest where the job involves immediate hands-on tasks that are completed within the working shift so that little needs to be handed on to the partner. This could apply to, say, customer service jobs where you are dealing with queries or complaints from the public, or to teaching where specific topics or lessons are covered within each session. Alternatively, job-sharing could work well where a job can be split into discrete parts – for example, separate research projects or managing separate staff.

People most suited to job-sharing

By definition, job-sharing involves working as a team, so if you are entering this type of arrangement you need to be a team player, in other words: co-operative, adaptable, willing to listen, willing to compromise, a good communicator, willing to share both credit and blame, and with a sense of responsibility to the job-share partner.

You also need to be good at planning and organising. The reason for this is twofold: first, you should be capable of getting your share of the job done in the agreed time so that you are not dumping your undone tasks on your partner; secondly, you will need to manage the handover of work between you.

You might need to be relaxed about being called when you are away from work. This is because, depending on the nature of the job, urgent issues might crop up that your partner can't deal with if they concern your parts of the job.

Job-sharing would not be a good move for anyone who is a bit of a loner, overly ambitious, unwilling to share the glory, a poor communicator, poor time-manager, or someone who lacks respect for their colleagues.

Beyond the personal qualities, people who have experienced job-shares usually point out the need for the partners to have a real empathy for each other and ability to develop shared goals for the job. This means that a job-share that works very well for you with one partner could fail if the partner changed.

Coming and going

Employers that have a job-share policy generally take either or both of two approaches to setting up a job-share:

- two employees must match themselves and jointly apply to fill a post or convert an existing job into a share, and/or
- a single employee can request a job-share and the employer will advertise for a partner. The original job-share applicant might then be involved in some way in the recruitment of the partner. However, if no job-share partner comes forward, the job-share cannot go ahead.

Once a job-share has been established, one partner might decide to leave (or be dismissed). What happens to the remaining partner depends on the particular job and employer. The possibilities are:

- a new partner is recruited and the job-share continues
- no new partner is found and the remaining partner carries on working part-time. The danger here is that your employer might either negligently or unwittingly pile some of the lost partner's work on to you
- no new partner is found and you are invited to carry on in the post but on a full-time basis. If you are not willing to do this, your employer might be able to offer you another job. If there is no job you want to take up, your employer might have justifiable grounds for making you redundant.

Financial aspects of working part-time or job-sharing

Impact on your income and spending

Working part-time will clearly reduce your income. The reduction will not be in the same proportion to the hours shed because tax is highest on the last slices of your pay. Based on very simple tax affairs (for someone with just the personal allowance and no fringe benefits or allowable expenses), Table 5.1 shows that if, say, you halve your hours and so halve your gross pay, the reduction in take-home pay could be closer to just two-fifths. If you cut your hours and gross pay by a third, the drop in take-home pay could be around a quarter. But this effect is more pronounced for people on lower earnings. So, at higher earnings, cutting your hours by, say, half produces a near halving of your take-home pay.

But once you also take into account savings on work-related costs – for example, travelling and childcare – the overall reduction in the income you have left over after all work-related deductions could be much smaller than the drop in your gross pay. In particular, if you have a very young family and need to hire childcare for all the hours you are at work, you might find that cutting your working hours leaves you no worse off overall.

Another aspect of working fewer hours and earning less is that you might be eligible to newly claim working tax credit or to claim more in tax credits than before. See Chapter 11 for a description of how working tax credit works and who is eligible and Table 5.2 below.

If you will find it hard to manage on your reduced income, take a look at Chapter 9 for ideas on how to control spending and possibly increase your income.

Impact on your pension

This section describes the main impact of working part-time or job-sharing on your various pensions. For details of how the pension systems work, see Chapter 12.

Table 5.1 How cutting your hours might affect take-home pay*

Your full-time pay		Part-time pay if you halve your hours				Part-time pay if you cut your hours by a third			
Before tax and National Insurance	Take-home pay after tax and National Insurance	Before tax and National Insurance	Take-home pay after tax and National Insurance	Fall in gross pay	Fall in take-home pay	Before tax and National Insurance	Take-home pay after tax and National Insurance	Fall in gross pay	Fall in take-home pay
£10,000	£8,508	£5,000	£4,946	50%	42%	£6,667	£6,275	33%	26%
£15,000	£11,858	£7,500	£6,833	50%	42%	£10,000	£8,508	33%	28%
£20,000	£15,208	£10,000	£8,508	50%	44%	£13,333	£10,742	33%	29%
£25,000	£18,558	£12,500	£10,183	50%	45%	£16,667	£12,975	33%	30%
£30,000	£21,908	£15,000	£11,858	50%	46%	£20,000	£15,208	33%	31%
£40,000	£28,742	£20,000	£15,208	50%	47%	£26,667	£19,675	33%	32%
£50,000	£34,642	£25,000	£18,558	50%	46%	£33,333	£24,303	33%	30%
£60,000	£40,542	£30,000	£21,908	50%	46%	£40,000	£28,742	33%	29%
£70,000	£46,442	£35,000	£25,586	50%	45%	£46,667	£32,676	33%	30%
£80,000	£52,342	£40,000	£28,742	50%	45%	£53,333	£36,609	33%	30%
£90,000	£58,242	£45,000	£31,692	50%	46%	£60,000	£40,542	33%	30%
£100,000	£64,142	£50,000	£34,642	50%	46%	£66,667	£44,476	33%	31%

* Figures for 2004–5 tax year.

Table 5.2 Examples of the maximum tax credits you might be able to claim*

Household income	Single person with no children	Couple with no children	Couple or single parent with one child	Couple or single parent with two children
£5,000	£1,570	£3,115	£10,019	£13,830
£10,000	£0	£1,287	£8,191	£12,002
£15,000	£0	£0	£6,341	£10,152
£20,000	£0	£0	£4,491	£8,302
£25,000	£0	£0	£2,641	£6,452
£30,000	£0	£0	£791	£4,602
£40,000	£0	£0	£545	£902
£50,000	£0	£0	£545	£545
£60,000	£0	£0	£0	£0

* Amounts for 2004–5 tax year. Assumes you work at least 16 hours but less than 30 hours a week and, where applicable, can claim the maximum childcare element of working tax credit.

State pension

Provided you continue to earn at least as much as the lower earnings limit (£79 a week in 2004–5), you will continue to build up state basic pension.

At present, the state additional pension is earnings-related, so a drop in your earnings could mean you build up a smaller pension (assuming you are not in any case contracted out – see page 223). However, under the special rules that protect low earners, if you earn at least the lower earnings limit but less than the low earnings threshold (£11,600 in 2004–5), you will build up state additional pension as if your earnings were at that level.

Occupational pension

Part-timers – including job-sharers – may not be treated less favourably than equivalent full-time workers. Therefore you have the right to join or remain in any occupational pension scheme open to other employees at your workplace.

However, in a final salary scheme (see page 228), benefits are normally scaled back pro rata if you work part-time. (So, for example, if you earn half the salary of an equivalent full-time employee, you build up pension at half the rate.)

In a money purchase scheme (see page 228), both your own and your employer's contributions are normally set as a percentage of your pay. So, if you are earning less, there will be a reduction in the amount being paid into the scheme for you and your ultimate pension will be smaller.

If you can afford to, consider making extra pension contributions to top up your pension – see page 232.

Personal pensions

Any personal pension or stakeholder scheme that you have will continue but, because of the fall in your income, you might not be able to afford to pay in as much which will ultimately mean a lower pension.

Nearly everyone can pay £3,600 a year into personal pensions and stakeholder schemes. If you are earning, often you can pay in more depending on your age and earnings. The reduction in earnings as a result of going part-time might mean that you have to cut back your pension contributions in order to stay within the Inland Revenue rules. However, the rules are due to change from 2006 – see page 239.

Stakeholder schemes are very flexible, so there will be no problem if you have to reduce or suspend your contributions. Older personal pensions are often not so flexible. Before cutting the amount you pay in or stopping contributions altogether, check with the provider how ongoing charges will affect your plan.

Further information

To find out more about your legal rights at work, see the free leaflets listed in Table 5.3.

If you belong to an occupational pension scheme, before deciding to switch to job-sharing or working part-time, contact your pensions administrator★ to discuss the possible impact on your eventual pension.

Table 5.3 Free leaflets about your rights at work

Leaflet/booklet reference	Title	Where from?
none	*Factsheet for part-timers*	Department of Trade and Industry*
03/624	*Flexible working. A guide for employers and employees*	Department of Trade and Industry*
PL516	*The right to apply to work flexibly*	Department of Trade and Industry*
none	*Employment tribunals*	Department of Trade and Industry*
none	*Flexible working: new rights for parents*	Equal Opportunities Commission*
none	*Flexible working: your rights*	Equal Opportunities Commission*
none	*Code of practice: sex discrimination*	Equal Opportunities Commission*

Chapter 6

Telecommuting and working from home

> This chapter looks at *employees* working from home. If you are thinking of running your own business from home, see Chapter 7.

If your employer agrees to your working from home either all the time or on a regular basis, this can be an ideal way to combine work and family responsibilities. It can also suit anyone who is looking for a more flexible approach to work.

According to a study by the University of Bradford, employees working from home often have better personal relationships, for example, with their partner and they are more likely to get involved in their local community. Employers can also benefit: the study also found that firms which allow employees to work from home at least some of the time tend to report higher productivity and lower absenteeism.

However, working mainly from home will not suit everyone. You might miss contact with your colleagues. You'll find it hard if you lack the discipline to get on with the job or conversely to shut up shop at the end of your working day. And you'll need a suitable space from which to work, ideally a separate room.

Rachel's story

Rachel had been thinking about downshifting for a couple of years so that she could spend more time with her husband, who is retired, and her parents who live some distance away. *'I read all the books I could find on the subject. However, most of these focused on moving to a rural area and starting a home-based business, often smallholding-related. They did not generally cover my idea of reduced hours, less pressure and more control, while still having a challenging career.'*

She had attended a career review course which had helped her identify the area she wanted to work in and, as a first step, she set about obtaining the vocational qualifications and professional membership she needed. Major changes at work, causing long hours and stress, accelerated Rachel's plans and she started to hunt for a new job.

'I started to search through the Internet and newspapers and other publications. The job I now have was only the second I applied for and seemed "meant to be". It was a very good fit for my idea of the ideal job.'

Rachel now works as a 'performance specialist', undertaking projects to help organisations improve their performance. The job advertisement highlighted flexible and family-friendly working arrangements. It offered full-time work or the employee's preferred pattern of part-time work, such as short days and term-time working. It also promised the opportunity to work at home when not required in the office for meetings or project work with clients.

Rachel chose to work part-time four days a week with a set day off *'although I agreed to be flexible about working on my day off when necessary and taking the time off in lieu'*. After a settling-in period, she is now free to work from home whenever she wishes rather than in the office.

'The job fits my career plan. It offers a halfway house to being self-employed and a good level of flexibility and control over my working life without all the workload uncertainties of self-employment. It also provided an opportunity to learn new skills and experience which would be very valuable if I moved on to take that next step.'

Rachel is enthusiastic about the impact downshifting has had on her life: *'The job itself is everything I wanted. I am challenged and stretched but in control of my working day and no longer bogged down by emails and wall-to-wall meetings. My working days are shorter, the long daily commute is gone. I am healthier and happier. The basket of anti-stress remedies I used to use went immediately. My husband is the one who best sums up what downshifting has done for me and us: he tells everyone it's like having a new wife. One who is more relaxed and happy without signs of constant stress.'*

Who works from home?

According to a study published by the Economic and Social Research Council (ESRC) in 2000, around a quarter of the UK labour force work at least *sometimes* from home – see Table 6.1 – though the proportion working *mainly* or completely from home is much smaller at only 2.5 per cent. The totals include people running their own business as well as employees. Not surprisingly, if you are an employee, you are more likely to work sometimes or partially from home than the whole time. For example, your presence at the office or other site is still likely to be required for meetings.

The most likely types of employee to work sometimes from home are categorised as managers, administrators and professionals. They include people who are, for example, teachers, lecturers, accountants, solicitors, doctors, nurses, scientists, lab technicians, computer analysts and people working in the media.

Of those working mainly from home, skilled craft and related jobs, such as builders, plumbers and electricians, are most prevalent – but most of these are self-employed. Employees working mainly from home are often in low-paid, unskilled jobs, including traditional homeworkers recruited by firms to assemble or package goods such as clothing and electrical items.

Whitehall

Tessa is a senior civil servant in Whitehall. She's worked from home one day a week for the past 22 years, during which time she's gained four promotions. *'Flexible working arrangements were forced upon me by unexpected circumstances. I joined the Civil Service as an executive officer at 21 but in my mid-twenties, as a higher executive officer, I developed rheumatoid arthritis. I soon found that I couldn't cope with the job, the illness and the commuting. But I was loath to give up the positive element of this – my job. Personnel were enormously supportive and agreement was reached which let me work from home for one day a week with a laptop to help me ... It has been a great benefit to me and to the department. I rarely become so debilitated by RA that I have to have sick leave. I work very effectively at home, leaving the difficult or creative tasks for the relative quiet of the work-at-home days.'*

Source: Department of Trade and Industry* Work–Life Balance website

Co-operative Bank

The Co-operative Bank in Manchester employs teleworkers in its Managed Accounts team. By working from home, teleworkers save on office clothes, travelling time and costs. The bank benefits from staff retention and increased productivity. Kirsty has worked for the Co-operative Bank for 15 years. She lives 35 miles from the bank's office in Manchester and used to spend three hours a day travelling to and from work. But since 1995 she's been teleworking. *'I applied to do telework and was given psychometric tests and interviewed to see if I'd be suited to working at home. I work a 35-hour week and I'm the team coach for all the teleworkers. I help them develop skills so they can move through the bank as they wish.'* All the teleworkers are still part of the Managed Accounts team and go into the bank once a month. *'We teleworkers are treated exactly as we would be if we were in the office. When I worked I didn't have a social life in the week and often didn't see my husband because he works in the evenings. The travel was particularly stressful. Now I don't feel so tired all the time. I can even walk the dog before I start work each morning. By not travelling to Manchester, I've saved money. I've sold my car, and saved on clothes for work and food. I know I'm much more productive because there are no interruptions. I think the bank gains too because it retains staff. It takes years before people are fully experienced. Training them to that point is very expensive. If they leave they take the knowledge with them. Costs for setting up employees with home work stations has been significantly lower than buying additional office space.'*

Source: Department of Trade and Industry* Work–Life Balance website.

Not everyone who works from home is a 'teleworker'. The government has in recent years started to gather statistics on the number of 'teleworkers', defined as people who in their main job work mainly or occasionally from home and could not do so without using a phone and computer. This will include many of the managers, administrators and professionals working from home. The government research suggests that on this definition around 4 per cent of all employees and self-employed people (around 1 million) were teleworkers in the year 2000. Using a wider definition, the ESRC research found that three out of five people who worked at home sometimes or partially (around 4 million) were reliant on communications technology to keep in touch with their workplace and colleagues. This applied to less than half of the people who worked mainly from home.

Table 6.1 UK workers working from home in 1998

Time spent working from home	Number	Percentage of those working from home who are:		
		Men	Women	Employees
Mainly at home	680,612	30.7%	69.3%	32.0%
Partially at home	932,364	63.8%	36.2%	67.3%
Sometimes from home	5,864,379	62.9%	37.1%	75.9%
Employed workforce* as a whole	26,947,448	55.3%	44.7%	86.9%

Source: Economic and Social Research Council (ESRC) *Future of Work* Working Paper 4, March 2000.

*Employees (i.e. working for an employer), self-employed and unpaid family workers.

Legal aspects of working from home

Health and safety

Even though you are working from home, your employer is still responsible for your health and safety. Most of the same regulations that apply in a normal workplace also apply to your home as a place of work.

Your employer is required to make an assessment of the risks and hazards you face doing your work at home and to take steps to prevent them causing harm. The assessment should be repeated from time to time.

An assessment involves considering the risks that you, your family and visitors to your home might face. To do this, your employer might need to visit your home. Alternatively, you might be asked to identify the risks. Your employer needs to assess who might be harmed, so needs to know if, say, you have children.

Depending on the nature of your work, the sort of things your employer might need to consider include:

- the risk of tripping over flexes
- the appropriateness and safety of equipment you use from home
- the safe use and storage of any hazardous substances
- minimising health problems associated with lifting heavy or awkward loads, doing repetitive tasks, using computers, and so on.

If you are pregnant or have recently given birth, your employer must consider the health and safety of the child as well as you.

Your employer must equip you at home with first aid provisions appropriate to the type of work you do.

Planning permission

Even though you are an employee, you might still need planning permission to work from home. This is unlikely to be the case if your work is unobtrusive and does not involve major alterations to the building. But you will need permission if your work causes a change in the residential character of your home or part of it. This might be the case if, for example, the work involves:

- converting part of your home (say, a spare room or garage) into an office or workshop to such an extent that it is no longer suitable for residential use
- a significant increase in traffic
- a significant increase in people visiting your home
- storing goods or parking business vehicles at your home, or
- creating noise or smells.

Restrictions in mortgages and tenancy agreements

Your mortgage lender might require you to tell it if you intend to work from home – check your terms and conditions. Similarly, you might need permission from your landlord before you can work from home. However, in practice, if your work is low profile, it is unlikely that anyone would notice or object.

Insurance

Working from home might invalidate your buildings or contents insurance. For example, some policies contain exclusions stating that claims will be refused if they stem: *'directly or indirectly from the employment, business or profession of any member of your household'*. Check your policy wording. If there is a problem, contact your insurer who will probably be willing to extend cover though possibly for an extra charge. Ask your employer to reimburse any increase in premium.

Your employer should make sure that any equipment belonging to your employer that you use in your work is properly insured both at your home and in transit between home and your employer's premises. But discuss this with your employer to make sure the appropriate cover is taken out.

If you use a car for business, the arrangements will be the same as for employees who are based at their employer's office. So, if your firm provides a company car or use of a pool car, it will be your employer who arranges the insurance. If you use your own car on business, it will be up to you to ensure that your insurance policy covers you for this and your employer may well pay you a mileage allowance which is generally based on total business motoring costs including something towards insurance.

Business rates

Anyone who occupies business premises normally has to pay business rates and, where a property has shared business–private residence use, business rates are due in respect of the business part of the property and council tax in respect of the rest. The same treatment may apply where you use part of your home for business purposes – which includes employees working from home – but this is decided on a case-by-case basis.

Until recently, whether business rates should be due has been a grey area with the authorities often taking a hard line and levying some rates on a proportional basis even where a room in the home was used only partly for work and also for some domestic purposes.

However, in 2003, an important tribunal case (Tully vs. Jorgensen) clarified the matter. The case concerned an Inland Revenue employee working from home and the judge ruled that, where home-based work involves using furniture and equipment normally found in a home, residential use is not compromised and business rates are not payable. But, if for example you make structural alterations to your home, use specialist equipment and/or have customers visiting your home, this could justify a charge for business rates.

Financial aspects of working from home

Impact on your income

The ESRC survey (see page 92) found that employees working from home on average earn more than those who do not work from home – see Table 6.2. But the totals hide some large discrepancies.

Around a quarter of people who work mainly from home are in low-paid jobs, usually manual, and nine-tenths of these are women. The average pay of manual employees working from home is just £2.86 an hour compared with £5.49 for manual workers who do not work from home. Some from this low-paid group are traditional 'homeworkers'.

If you are an employee aged 18 or over, bear in mind that you are entitled to receive at least a minimum wage (£4.85 an hour from October 2004) if you are aged 22 or over. (Lower rates apply to younger workers.) Homeworkers can instead be paid a 'fair piece rate' which has in the past resulted in many receiving less than the minimum wage. From October 2004 and 2005 new regulations are being introduced which should ensure that homeworkers do actually get the minimum wage. However, many traditional homeworkers are outside the protection of the minimum wage because they are classified as self-employed not employees (see Chapter 7).

Where you work from home, you should not expect to be paid any less than colleagues doing a similar job from your employer's premises. Bear in mind that when you work from home your employer may well save money on, for example, electricity and phone bills and, if you work mainly from home, on desk space too. By the same token, you are likely to be running up work-related expenses at home.

Table 6.2 Average pay of UK workers working from home in 1998

Time spent working from home	Average hourly pay rate for employees
Mainly at home	£10.85
Partially at home	£13.28
Sometimes from home	£12.01
Employed workforce as a whole	£7.79

Source: Economic and Social Research Council (ESRC) *Future of Work* Working Paper 4, March 2000.

Impact on your spending

Working regularly from home might save you money. For example, you might save on travelling costs and lunches. If you work completely from home, there might be other savings on, say, clothing for work. On the other hand, your home-related expenses are likely to increase, for example, what you spend on heating and lighting. If you use the phone, email or Internet a lot, your phone bill will be higher too.

Your employer might reimburse the extra costs you run up working from home. Since 6 April 2003, you do not have to pay tax on money you get from your employer for this purpose provided you are working at home under a formal arrangement with your employer. If the amount you are paid is no more than £104 a year, you get this tax relief without having to provide any documentation to show what your extra household costs are. If you receive a higher amount, you will have to give your employer records to back up the claim. For example, you can pick out work-related calls from an itemised phone bill and fuel bills for the periods before and after you started to work from home may show how their cost has increased.

If you run up extra costs working from home but your employer does not reimburse them, you might be able to claim tax relief on what you have paid out yourself. But in many cases, you will not be eligible for such tax relief because it is not enough that you incurred the expenses wholly and exclusively for work and in performing your duties as an employee. In addition it must be necessary for you to work from home. In deciding this, the Inland Revenue considers whether it is necessary for any employee in your position – not you specifically – to work from home and the tax relief claim would be denied if you could have done the work from elsewhere – say, a public library.

However, the tax system does offer some other limited encouragement to employees working from home. Most fringe benefits that you get through a job are taxable, but some are tax-free. For example, your employer can lend you computer equipment without this counting as a taxable benefit even though the computer is available for your private use as well as work. You can also have a mobile phone from work tax-free.

If you are able to convince the Inland Revenue that it is necessary for you to work from home, you might be able to claim tax relief for a wider range of expenses, for example, the costs of travelling between home and other workplaces. See 'Further information' (overleaf).

Impact on your pension

If you were originally taken on for a job at your employer's premises, there is no change to your contract of employment simply because you switch to doing some or all of your job from home. Therefore, there should be no change to the pensions you are building up whether through the state scheme, an occupational scheme or personal pensions.

There is some speculation that people who work mainly from home and so have little contact with colleagues in their workplace might be overlooked when it comes to promotion. If that is true, the resultant lower earnings would normally cause a knock on reduction in the state additional pension and any occupational pension.

As discussed above, traditional homeworking is typically very low-paid work. If you earn less than £79 a week in 2004–5 (assuming you count as an employee), you will not be building up any state pension (basic or additional). Membership of an occupational pension scheme is unlikely to be offered with this type of work. If you can afford to, you could arrange your own personal pension or stakeholder scheme.

See Chapter 12 for more information about the different types of pension scheme and how they work.

Further information

Your contract of employment might include a right to work at least part of the time from home. If not, you'll need to negotiate with your employer. Some employers have formal policies to cover homeworking.

Before you start to work from home, check what home-related expenses your employer will cover and the tax position with the payroll or accounts department at work. Also get the following free guides from the Inland Revenue★: 480 *Expenses and benefits – a tax guide* and 490 *Employee travel – a tax and NICs guide for employers*.

The Health and Safety Executive★ publish several free booklets that may be useful: *Homeworking. Guidance for employers and employees on health and safety*, *Basic advice on first aid at work* and *A guide for new and expectant mothers who work*. See also *Telework guidance: as agreed by the TUC, CBI and CEEP UK*, available from the Department of Trade and Industry★.

If there is a possibility that the work will change the residential nature of your home or cause disruption to your neighbours, contact your local planning authority★ to find out if you will need planning permission and check that your mortgage lender or landlord agrees to your working from home.

Chapter 7

Becoming your own boss

For some, the ideal downshift is to escape the corporate culture and run their own business. The attraction is being able to control one's own life, the flexibility to choose one's own hours and perhaps to swap a barren urban backdrop for more congenial surroundings.

It can work out that way, but running your own business can also be challenging, demanding, time consuming and stressful. Crucial will be your choice of business and your ability to contain it within the confines you have set.

There are various options for running a business. At its simplest, you could opt for self-employment, operating either as a sole trader or in partnership with other people. This is the least formal business structure and often especially well-suited to smaller businesses, for example, where you are turning a craft-based hobby, such as pottery, jewellery-making or carpentry, into a paying concern, or you are selling your personal skills, for example, as a hairdresser, decorator, gardener, handyman or -woman, accountant, solicitor, proofreader or writer. The biggest drawback is that there is no protection for your personal assets if your business collapses (in other words, no 'limited liability'), so this is not the best structure for larger or more complex businesses. And there are also tax advantages which mean that even small businesses are often financially better off operating as companies rather than self-employed. See page 110 for a detailed look at the pros and cons of self-employment versus being a company.

If you are thinking of letting out property (say, a holiday home or caravan) or taking in lodgers, see Chapter 10. But if you intend to run a bed and breakfast, that counts as a business so read this chapter.

You do not have to start up your own business from scratch. Other options are to buy a business that is already up and running –

for example, take over a shop complete with stock and existing customer base – or perhaps buy a franchise. A franchise is the right to operate a business that uses somebody else's business idea and format. A wide variety of businesses are available on a franchise basis, for example, convenience stores, print shops, private home meal delivery services, greeting card distributors, personal care services, accountancy and tax services, plumbing, lock-fitting, commercial cleaning, hairdressing, children's music clubs, maths tuition, executive recruitment, private investigators, children's books supply, diet clubs, sign makers, photo developing and printing, and supplying

---

Patrick's story

Patrick took early retirement on health grounds at the age of 53. He had an early full pension and was able to plan a limited lifestyle based on that. After a lengthy convalescence, he decided to work again. '*I am now a qualified, professional genealogist, which is most fun. I am also an independent education adviser supporting families, a career which appears unique but is much valued by my clients.*'

Starting up was not all roses: '*I had assumed that, because I had found two niches, the work would flow in. But because my advice work is in a brand new area, there is considerable mistrust about whether it is a worthwhile investment for parents (although my results confirm it is). I have to work hard to create an image, but most of my work comes in from word of mouth.*'

The business has now become established but perversely that creates another difficulty: '*For the past two months, it is apparent that I have passed a critical point and word of mouth now delivers more work than I wish to take on. This is becoming a new problem – but a welcome one!*'

Throughout Patrick has set himself some strict rules of work: '*I work never more than three days a week (broken this month for the first time because of demand); I don't do work I dislike or for clients I dislike; I don't do meetings, management or paperwork, except directly relating to the task; I try to spend my earnings by the end of the year.*'

office plants. See page 107 for more about how franchising works. However, if you do buy an existing business or franchise, do not forget that your central motive is to downshift. Many existing businesses and most franchises are not part-time ventures. To make a success of them will often require your whole attention and long working hours. You will need to restrict your search only to those businesses that will give you the flexibility of choosing when and how long you work.

Another possibility is to become an agent for a home shopping company, selling anything from plastic storage containers to costume jewellery, from cleaning products to cosmetics, from books to saucy underwear. Typically this involves distributing catalogues, and/or organising parties at which you display and demonstrate the goods, collecting payment, channelling orders and delivering goods when they arrive. This form of business can be ideal for downshifting because you can normally choose how many or how few hours you work and when. But the drawback is that you will not necessarily earn much. See page 108 for more information.

Beware of homeworking scams which seemingly offer business opportunities that promise huge earnings for scant amounts of work – see page 109.

Starting from scratch

Your choice of business

Assuming you will be reliant at least partially on the income from your business, you will want it to be a success. Therefore, you need to choose the type of business carefully. It must be in an area where you feel you have particular skills or advantages.

One possibility is to continue with the type of work that you do now. This has the advantage that you have existing expertise and probably a network of contacts who might be a source of work and/or a resource you can use in it carrying out. You might, like Jane (see page 106), find that your former employer is your first client and so helps you to get your business up and running (though beware of 'IR35' – see page 122).

Similarly, basing your business on hobbies that you already have also might draw on existing expertise and contacts.

If you turn to a completely different area of work, you need to think about how you will acquire the necessary skills and expertise. Particularly, if you are choosing a largely unskilled area, you need to carefully probe why you think your business will succeed, for example:

- what stops other people setting up competing businesses? Maybe there are barriers to entry such as the need to invest in expensive equipment – can you afford this? Or perhaps you have a unique idea, but how will you stop others copying it? Is this something you can patent? Bear in mind getting a patent could take some time
- if there are competitors, why will customers come to you instead of others? Are you intending to charge less? This can be a dangerous strategy if it sparks a price war and low prices make it hard or impossible to achieve reasonable profits.
- is there a lack of this product or service locally? Why is this? Perhaps there is no demand or maybe potential customers already buy by, say, mail order or Internet and would not necessarily switch to you.

If you do have a unique idea, bear in mind that – as Patrick (see page 102) found – initially there might not be any demand for your product or service. You may have to educate customers about it before they realise they want to buy. The implications of this are either that you must be prepared for your business to grow only slowly at the start or that you will have to spend a lot on promoting your idea in addition to any promotion of the product or service itself.

If the business is to fulfil your ambition of downshifting, it will also need some special characteristics:

- the work itself must not take up all of your time
- the business must not generate too many additional tasks (such as administration, book-keeping and so on) or it must generate enough income so that you can pay others to do these jobs
- ideally, you should be able to control when the work is done – for example, it might be hard to keep time for yourself if you have a shop or office which customers expect to be open during normal business hours
- it must be possible to cap any tendency for the business to grow without damaging its existing viability.

Testing your idea

Whatever idea you settle on, it is crucial that you thoroughly investigate the viability of your proposed business before you start. You need to draw up a business plan to give you a clear picture of how you expect the business to develop during its first few years.

A business plan will be essential if you will be asking other people to invest in your business or lend to it. But, even if you have enough money to get started without outside help, you should still prepare a business plan. It will alert you to areas of weakness so that you can address them, and it will give you a baseline against which to track your progress. Hopefully, your business will flourish but, if not, comparing what happens in practice with the forecasts in your business plan will serve as an early warning system if things do start to go wrong. You may then be able to avert a potential crisis by taking steps to get back on track.

Your business plan should include:

- **a summary of the business**: what it does, description of the market, who the target customers are, the targets you have set for the business, why the business is expected to succeed and over what time frame
- **structure of the business**: its legal form (for example, sole trader, limited liability company), who the key people are, what skills they bring and what skills are weak or lacking
- **the product or service**: what it is, why people will buy it and who your competitors are
- **production details**: where you will be based, what equipment you'll use, what supplies you need, where will you get them, what staff you will need and where you will recruit them
- **marketing**: who your target customers are, how many potential customers there are, what proportion of the market you expect to take up your product, how you will price the product or service, how customers will get to hear about it, what your main marketing message will be and how you will deliver the product or service to customers – for example, face-to-face sales, mail order, Internet, through shops, agents and so on
- **financial analysis**: forecasts of your cash flow and profits for at least the first two or three years on a month-by-month basis. Forecast of your balance sheet at the end of each of those years.

Jane's story

Jane left full-time employment when she was expecting her second child. At the same time, she and her partner moved out of London to the countryside. *'This was a much more relaxed and friendly atmosphere in which to bring up children.'*

As a writer, Jane knew she could carry on making some money from freelance work, but the aim was to cut back and spend more time with the children while they were young. *'My full-time job was demanding. I had a nanny to look after my daughter so she was well cared for, but I felt I had too little time with her and this would only get worse when the second child arrived. Also trying to give 110 per cent to work and 110 per cent to family was causing major exhaustion.'*

Jane found it very easy to start up on her own because her previous employer was keen for her to carry on with some projects after she had left and she already had a network of contacts working for various publications and other organisations, so quickly built up a wide base of different clients. *'This is important. Although time constraints mean you physically can't manage too many clients, being reliant on just one or two is risky, because if they are slow to pay, fail, or their work dries up for some other reason, you lose a big chunk of your income.'*

Initially, the main financial outlay was just a good computer, books, stationery and subscriptions to various journals.

'The freelance business was reasonably small at first and, even when it did make big time demands, I could shift the hours I worked so I was always able to pick up the children, attend school assemblies and do lots of things with the children during the day.'

'The main problem has been trying to stop the business growing. I have never advertised and work comes in purely from existing clients, recommendation or as a result of new clients seeing my published work. In theory, you can always say "no" to a client. But, if you do that, they might find someone else who gets both that project and, even worse, follow-on work. So the tendency is always to say "yes" if you can, which can cause big peaks of work which are stressful and definitely not compatible with downshifting!'

Statement of the assumptions you have used to make the forecasts (for example, regarding rate of sales growth, interest rates, staff productivity). Risk analysis identifying all the potential threats to your success with estimates of how likely they are to arise, impact they might have, steps you can take to minimise the risks (for example, taking out insurance), and cost of taking those steps.

In addition, if you will want to raise outside finance, you will need to include a section showing what return your investors or lenders are expected to get out of backing you and over what time frame.

The business plan is such a crucial step in developing your idea in a sound and logical way, that you should take your time doing it and get professional help. In England, Business Link★, a government-sponsored organisation that aims to act as a single gateway for business information and advice, can direct you to sources to help you with the planning stage of your business. The equivalent organisations in the rest of the UK are Business Eye★ in Wales, Scottish Enterprise★, Highlands and Islands Enterprise★ and Invest Northern Ireland★.

Buying a franchise

A franchise is the right to operate someone else's business idea usually in a particular geographical area: normally you would expect to have an exclusive right so that you have the only such franchise in that area. The advantage of choosing a franchise is that you should be buying into a business idea or process that is already tried and tested and shown to work. You get to use a brand name that should already be widely known and respected. This means you by-pass the time and effort it takes to develop an idea and get established and hopefully reduce the risk of failure.

But this time-, labour- and risk-saving comes at a price. It's impossible to generalise, but you might have to pay anything from, say, £50,000 upwards as a lump sum in order to buy the franchise and there will be ongoing yearly fees as well (typically set as a percentage of your turnover).

In return for these fees, the person or firm selling you the franchise (the 'franchisor') might provide existing premises (or this may be down to you), will definitely provide the blueprint for operating the business normally in the form of a manual, should provide training, and should continue to market the brand as a whole. There may also be other commitments, such as updating the product, providing retraining, dealing with problems, and so on.

If the product or service involves equipment or supplies, you will normally have to buy these from the franchisor. You might have to pay more than you would have to if you were free to shop around for your own suppliers, so this could be a further, hidden charge.

The rights and obligations of you and the franchisor will be set out in the franchise agreement and it is essential that you fully understand this document before going ahead. You should hire a solicitor★ to help you do this.

You will need to assess whether the franchise offers a viable business opportunity and that the price being asked is fair. This will involve examining the franchisor's financial records, so you will probably want the help of an accountant★. You need to satisfy yourself that the franchisor will stick to the agreement – for example, that the product will be advertised and in an effective manner. Can you talk to people who already have a franchise from this franchisor? What is their experience?

As a downshifter, you have an additional area to investigate. How much time is involved in running the franchise? Does that match the time you are prepared to give? Will operating the franchise at the level you would prefer generate enough income?

There are plenty of crooks out there willing to relieve you of a large lump sum in exchange for an empty idea, so make sure you deal only with a reputable franchisor. Stick to members or affiliates of the British Franchise Association (BFA)★. BFA members must have an established track record, must operate ethically and in accordance with good practice standards. The BFA also operates a low-cost complaints system if things do go pear-shaped.

Becoming a home shopping agent

In some respects, this is not dissimilar to a home-based retail franchise. You have the right to sell a firm's products typically within a particular geographical area – though you might not have an exclusive right, so could be competing with others. You might have to pay something for this right, though any upfront fee is usually fairly small – say, less than £100. You earn by receiving commission on each product you sell.

The major advantage for a downshifter of being a home shopping agent is flexibility. Typically, you choose how much time you want to spend working and when you work.

Beware of homeworking scams – see Box. To guard yourself against scams, stick to firms which are members of the Direct Selling Association (DSA)★. Its members abide by codes of practice both to protect consumers and covering their business conduct with agents and representatives. The latter code, for example, requires the firms to have proper contracts with agents, to provide adequate training and to pay commission promptly. The DSA's members include big home-shopping names, such as Amway, Avon, Betterware, Kleeneze, The Body Shop at Home and Usborne Books.

Homeworking scams

If you do not have a particular business idea in mind but fancy the idea of working from home, you might be attracted by the many ads and emails making claims like this: *'Be your own boss. Earn hundreds of £s a week. No experience required'*. Don't be fooled. Invariably these offers are scams.

According to the Department of Trade and Industry, at any time there are around 300 scams like this. They work in several ways but nearly always you have to send money upfront. This is usually to:

- buy the plan of the money-making scheme. But – surprise, surprise – the ingenious plan tells you to place similar ads to the one you saw and then sell photocopies of the plan to respondents, or
- pay for materials so you can make the money-spinning product which might be nothing more desirable than, say, plaster casts of whimsical animals. But either you are left to find customers for the product yourself or the scheme operator accepts your output only if it reaches a high enough standard which – however meticulous you are – it never does.

If you come across a scam like this, report it to your local Trading Standards Department★.

Setting up a business

Your business structure

There are two basic forms your business might take: you could be self-employed (or in partnership if there you intend to collaborate with someone else) or you could set up your own company. Table 7.1 summarises the main differences between the two forms.

Table 7.1 Self-employment vs. your own company

Aspect to consider	Self-employment	Your own company
Legal status	No distinction between your identity and that of the business.	Business has its own legal identity. You are an employee (as a director) and shareholder.
Who owns the profits?	You.	The company.
Who is responsible for debts of the business?	You.	The company. 'Limited liability' means your personal assets are not normally at risk but see opposite.
Who's involved?	Can be just you.	Under current law, must be at least two people as a sole director may not also be company secretary.
Ease of starting-up	Informal. Just start trading and tell Inland Revenue within three months of end of month you start up.	More complicated. Need to form the company or buy one off-the-shelf and register with Companies House before you can start trading.
Administration	Simplified accounting procedures – you could keep your own accounts but might prefer to use an accountant.	Formal procedures. You will almost certainly want to use an accountant (and fees will usually be higher than for a self-employed business). Accounts must be filed annually with Companies House.
How are profits taxed?	Profits are added to any other income you have and you are taxed as described in Chapter 11.	Company pays corporation tax on the profits and any salary paid to you is an allowable expense. You personally are taxed on any salary and dividends paid out by the company as described in Chapter 11.

Table 7.1 *continued*

Aspect to consider	Self-employment	Your own company
How much tax?	Generally tax is higher than if you operated as a company.	Tax is lower than if you were self-employed provided you pay yourself only a small salary and the rest in dividends.
Paying yourself	Simple – just draw money from the business.	Formal. The company pays you a salary (and must operate PAYE) and/or declares a dividend to shareholders.
Your expenses	Can claim tax relief for most expenses you incur in connection with the business.	Directors are employees and not all expenses will be claimable. Perks provided by the company are often taxable.
Pension	Limited choice of pension arrangements and limit on how much you can pay in – but rules are changing from April 2006 (see page 239).	Wider choice of pension arrangements and, with some, no cap on amount paid in but rules change from April 2006 (see page 239).

Many of the differences stem from the fact that, unlike a self-employed business (or share in a traditional partnership), a company has a separate legal identity from you. This means that money made by the company does not belong to you – it is either paid out to employees and creditors or what's left over belongs to the company's shareholders. You will probably be both an employee (as a director) and a shareholder, but the company must still follow formal procedures designed to protect all the possible stakeholders not just you.

A key advantage of operating as a company is limited liability. This means that, when the chips are down, all the assets of the company can be used to pay the company's debts but nothing more. So – in theory at least – the most you can lose is the money you have put into the company as shareholder. In practice, this protection can be somewhat illusory. First, directors can be held personally liable (and so lose their own assets) if they allow the company to carry on trading when they know it to be insolvent. Secondly, if you need to raise money for the business – say, from a bank – the lender will often insist on securing the loan against your personal assets, usually your home. In that case, if the company went bust and could not repay the loan, the lender could seize your home and sell it in order to recover its money.

Another big advantage of using a company structure in recent years has been the scope to reduce your tax bills (see below). Although the 2004 Budget contained measures to reduce these tax advantages, all but the smallest businesses can still be quids in by choosing a corporate structure.

The main advantage of self-employment is its simplicity. It is very easy to stop and start trading and, if you want to, it's often reasonably straightforward to handle your own accounting and tax affairs. By contrast, if you set up as a company, you will almost certainly need the services of professionals such as an accountant.

Note that, if you set up in partnership with someone else and opt for a traditional partnership, you can benefit from the same informality that applies to the self-employed. But, however well you get on with your partner(s) now, you will not necessarily always see eye to eye in future. Therefore, although not essential, it is important to have a formal partnership agreement setting out matters such as how decisions will be made, what happens if a partner wants to leave, how profits will be shared, and so on. Get a solicitor to draw up a proper agreement for you.

How to start up as self-employed

You just start trading. Within three months of the end of the month you start up, you must tell the Inland Revenue that you are in business. Do this by calling the Inland Revenue★ Newly Self Employed Helpline or filling in the form CWF1 in the back of leaflet P/SE1 *Thinking of working for yourself?* which is available from tax offices or the Inland Revenue★ website. If you fail to do this; you could be fined up to £100.

The Inland Revenue will log you into the National Insurance and income tax systems. It will also pass on your details if you need to or want to register for VAT.

There are relatively few restrictions on what you call your business but, as for companies (see below) the use of some words is restricted. For guidance, get booklet GBF3 *Business names* from Companies House★. If your business trades under a name that is not your own name, you must also display your name on your business stationery.

How to start up as a company

First you need to set up a company and register it with Companies House★. You can do this yourself, in which case contact Companies House for a starter pack containing guidance booklets and the forms you need. There is a small registration fee. Alternatively, you can get an accountant, solicitor or a firm specialising in company formations to set up your company for you or sell you a ready-made company, for which it will charge a fee.

With a ready-made company, you may want to change the company's name and this new name will have to be registered with Companies House. There is a fast-track service so you can set up a company in a day, but more usually it takes a week or two.

There are restrictions on the name you can choose for your company. Some words are prohibited or can be used only with permission from the government – they include, for example, 'British' and 'Royal'. You may not have a name which is already being used by another company – you'll need to check your proposed name against those registered already with Companies House.

Where you will work

Working from home

If your business is to be reasonably small, often an ideal arrangement will be to work from home because it keeps down costs. It may also fit nicely with downshifting if it means you can combine work and, say, family commitments. On the other hand, working from home can blur the divide between work and home life and ultimately threaten rather than support a better work–life balance.

If your work is unobtrusive – for example, it involves consultancy or administrative tasks – you can usually work from home without any special arrangements. However, if the business will involve adapting your home (say, building a workshop) noise, using hazardous chemicals, employing staff, a large number of suppliers and/or customers visiting your home, then you are likely to need planning permission from your local planning authority★ before you can go ahead. Permission will not necessarily be granted, though the planning department may be willing to give you an opinion on the likelihood of this before you put in an application.

If you are making something from home, you do not necessarily need to open up your premises to customers. You could sell by mail order, say, or by taking stalls at fairs and markets.

Bear in mind that, if applicable, you may need permission from your mortgage lender before starting to run a business from home. And your home might be subject to a restrictive covenant banning its use for business – this will be stated in your deeds if you own your home or in the lease if you are renting. Depending on the precise terms, your neighbours, landlord or even the developer from whom you bought the home might have the right to apply to the courts to enforce the restriction. However, in practice, if your work is low profile and does not inconvenience anyone, any action to stop you is unlikely. Nevertheless, if you rent, check with your landlord before starting a business from home.

Don't assume that your normal house insurance will cover a home-based business. Commonly, your building and contents policies specifically exclude claims relating to business use of your home so you should at least let your insurer know that you will be running a business from home. Usually, you can arrange, for an extra premium, an extension to a contents policy to cover business equipment. But a better option will normally be to arrange separate business cover which would also cover business interruption (lost profits following say a fire), employer's liability (which covers your responsibility for any employees injured while working), and so on. You can get combined home-business policies specifically designed for people running a own business from home.

See page 119 for guidance on tax if you work from home.

Working from business premises

The alternative to working from home is to have dedicated business premises. Where you choose depends very much on the nature of your business. If you are selling retail, you might need a shop, office or other outlet in an established shopping area. If your business involves arts and crafts, a small workshop might be the answer, perhaps in a specialist artists' enclave. If you will be building or manufacturing something, a workshop on a trading estate might be suitable.

If suppliers or customers will be visiting your premises, consider the sort of impression you want to project and choose premises that fit in with that. For example, if you are offering a professional service, such as accountancy, it may be important to have a reasonably smart office that projects competence and efficiency.

Having business premises inevitably costs more than working from home. In addition to rent or purchasing the premises, you will have to pay, for example, to heat and light the premises, business rates (regardless of whether you are making any profits), insurance premiums and probably security costs.

Tax if you run your own business

Tax if you are self-employed

The basics

Your business has no separate legal identity from you, so profits from your business are added to your other income for the tax year. Income tax is then worked out as described in Chapter 11.

As a self-employed person, you normally pay Class 2 and Class 4 National Insurance contributions as described on page 204 onwards.

Class 2 contributions are charged at a flat-rate and usually paid monthly by direct debit. Class 4 contributions and income tax are collected through the self-assessment system (see page 119).

What profits are taxed?

The profit from your business is broadly the revenues from selling your product or services less the costs you incur. So you deduct, for example, the cost of raw materials, the wages you pay employees, costs of running an office, what you pay for books and journals used in your business, cost of employing an accountant, bank charges and so on. If you run up business expenses before you start to trade, for tax purposes they are treated as if incurred on the first day of trading provided the expenses count as allowable under the normal tax rules.

For tax purposes, you start with your profits worked out according to generally accepted accounting principles (and you can buy guidance books or software to help you do this). However, to arrive at taxable profits, you make some adjustments.

In particular, some costs you deduct for your business accounts are not allowable deductions when working out your tax bill. The general rule is that to be allowable for tax any expense must be incurred *'wholly and exclusively'* for the purpose of your business. Applied strictly, this would mean that any expense that was incurred partly for non-business reasons would be completely disallowed. But, in practice, the Inland Revenue lets you claim part of a mixed business – private expense provided the business part can be clearly identified or measured. For example, you can claim part of your motoring costs where you use a car both privately and on business if you keep a record of all your costs and a log of your mileage with the business miles separately shown. The allowable part of the expense is then business miles/total mileage × total expenses. But you would not be allowed to claim the cost of a single trip during which you did some business but also stopped off to do some shopping and visit a friend because it is not possible to separate out the business element of the journey.

Another major difference between your business accounts and tax accounts is the treatment of spending on capital items. In both, you would not normally deduct the whole cost of something in the year you bought it if you expected to use the item in the business for many years. In your business accounts, you normally spread the cost over the expected life of the asset, deducting part of the cost each year as 'depreciation'. There are various ways of working this out but a common method is 'straight-line depreciation' where, say, if the item is expected to last five years you deduct one-fifth of the cost each year.

In your tax accounts, depreciation is not an allowable expense and you have to add it back to your profits. But instead you can deduct capital allowances. These are, if you like, depreciation worked out according to a standard set of rules, though the capital allowance system is also used by the government to encourage certain types of spending.

There are two types of capital allowance: first-year allowances and writing-down allowances. In the year you buy a capital item, you claim a first-year allowance. The cost less the allowance then goes into a pool and next year you claim a writing-down allowance up to 25 per cent of the value of the pool. The allowance is deducted from the pool and next year you claim a further 25 per cent of the balance, and so on.

Small businesses can generally claim first year allowances up to 50 per cent of the cost for items bought between 6 April 2004 and 5 April 2005. With some items, the first year allowance is 100 per cent

– in other words, you can claim the full cost in the year of purchase. This applies for example to many types of energy-saving equipment.

The 25, 50 and 100 per cent mentioned above are the maximum allowances available. You can claim less than the full amount and this is worth doing if your tax bill is already reduced to nothing by other allowances (for example, your personal allowance).

When your profits are taxed

Usually, you divide up the life of your business into accounting years. Normally your year will end on the same day each year and you choose your accounting year end.

Once your business has been going for a few years, you are taxed on a 'current year basis'. This means your bill for a tax year (which runs from 6 April to the following 5 April) is based on your profits for the accounting year which ends in that tax year. For example, if your accounting year end is 30 April, you will be taxed in the 2004–5 tax year on your profits for the accounting year ending on 30 April 2004.

In the first two or sometimes three years of business, the rules are different. In general, in your first year, you are taxed on your actual profits for the tax year (i.e. from the date of start up to 5 April). In the second year, you are usually taxed on profits for the first 12 months of trading. The profits for these periods are found by taking a proportion of your profits for the relevant accounting periods (see Example on page 118).

As you can see from the Example, these 'opening year rules' mean that some profits are taxed more than once. These are called 'overlap' profits. Eventually, you can claim tax relief back on these profits but not until your business closes (or, in some cases, earlier if you change your accounting year end). Because there is usually such a long delay until you get this relief, its value has normally been heavily eroded by inflation, so the relief may be fairly worthless.

You can avoid the complications of the opening year rules and avoid having any overlap profit if you opt for 'fiscal accounting'. This means aligning your accounting year with the tax year. You do not have to have a year end exactly on 5 April. You still qualify for fiscal accounting if your year end is, say, 31 March. With fiscal accounting, from the start, you are simply taxed each tax year on your profits for that year.

Since it is so simple, why doesn't everyone opt for fiscal accounting? The main drawback is that there is relatively little time between your year end and having to send in your tax return and pay the tax due (see page 199). For example, if your accounting year ends on 31 March 2004, you must send in your tax return and pay the balance of any tax bill by 31 January 2005, giving you ten months to get your accounts and other paperwork sorted out. If your accounting year ends on 30 April 2004, your tax return and balance of the tax bill are not due until 31 January 2006, giving you a much bigger breathing space of 22 months.

Example

Jack starts a business on 1 October 2004 and chooses an accounting year end of 30 April. He draws up his first accounts on 30 April 2005. During his first accounting period, he makes profits of £10,000. In his next accounting period ending 30 April 2006, he makes £18,000. His tax bills are worked out as follows:

Tax year	Basis for taxing profits	Profits which are taxed
2004–5	Actual profits from 1 October 2004 to 5 April 2005 (187 days)	187/212 × £10,000 = £8,820
2005–6	First 12 months of trading	212/212 × £10,000 + 153/365 × £18,000 = £17,545
2006–7	Normal current year basis	£18,000

Jack's first accounting period lasts 212 days, but he is taxed on (187 + 212) = 399 days' worth of that profit. The extra 187 days is called an overlap period and the extra 187/212 × £10,000 = £8,820 on which he pays tax is called overlap profit. Similarly, his second accounting period lasts 365 days but he is taxed on (153 + 365) = 518 days of profits. The extra 153 days is an overlap period and the extra 153/365 × £18,000 = £7,545 is overlap profit. So Jack carries forward overlap profit of £8,820 + £7,545 = £16,365 in total.

Losses

You might make a loss in your business at any time, but it is particularly likely in the early years when you are getting established. You can claim tax relief on losses and have a choice about how you get this relief. You can:

- carry losses forward indefinitely and deduct them from future profits from the same business
- set losses against income and then gains you have in the same tax year from other sources
- set losses against income and then gains you had in the previous tax year from other sources
- for losses made in the first four years of trading, set them against income from other sources in any of the preceding three tax years
- for losses made in the last 12 months before closing down, set them against profits made in the previous three years.

Tax if you are self-employed and work from home

Chapter 6 considers the tax position if you are an employee working from home – the expenses on which you can claim tax relief are very limited. By contrast, if you run your own business, you can claim any expenses provided they are incurred *'wholly and exclusively'* for business.

As described on page 115, this does not prevent you claiming the business part of some joint private-business costs. So, if you work from home, you can usually claim part of the household costs, such as heating and lighting, as a business expense. You take a proportion of the total costs commensurate to your business use, based on say the proportion of the floor area of your home given over to business use or the number of rooms used for business. You need to agree an appropriate basis with your tax office.

In general, you can't claim home-related costs that you would have to pay anyway even if you were not running a business from home, though the rules are not clear-cut. For example, if you have just one phone line, you can claim the cost of your business calls (identifiable from an itemised statement) but not a proportion of the line rental which you would have to pay anyway if the phone was wholly for private use. But, if you have a second line put in so that you can use one purely for business, you can claim the increase in rental in respect of the second line.

If you use part of your home exclusively for business, you can claim a suitable proportion of the interest on any mortgage as a business expense. But setting aside part of your home exclusively for business means that part will not be eligible for relief against capital gains tax when you come to sell (though it might be covered by your yearly allowance) – see page 202.

Working from home, you might have to pay business rates (in which case you should get some compensating reduction in your council tax). This used to be a grey area but was clarified by a tribunal case in 2003 (Tully v Jorgensen). The case concerned an Inland Revenue employee working from home but is equally valid for people running their own business from home. The judge ruled that, where home-based work involves using furniture and equipment normally found in a home, residential use is not compromised and business rates are not payable. But, if for example you make structural alterations to your home, use specialist equipment, have employees working from your home and/or have customers visiting your home, this could justify a charge for business rates.

Tax if you operate as a company

The company's tax bill

Your company, which has a separate tax identity from you, pays corporation tax on the profits of the business. The profits are worked out in much the same way as described above for a self-employed person. So, for example, an expense must be incurred 'wholly and exclusively' for the purpose of the business, depreciation is not allowable but capital allowances are, and so on.

Small companies are taxed fairly lightly. In 2004–5, a company with profits up to £50,000 pays no tax on the first £10,000 and 23.75 per cent on the next £40,000 (giving a maximum average tax rate of 19 per cent). A company with profits over £50,000 and up to £300,000 is taxed at the small companies' rate of 19 per cent on all its profits.

Your tax bill

As an owner-manager of the company, you are most likely both a director and a shareholder. As a director, you are an employee. What you are paid in salary is an allowable expense which the company can deduct when working out its taxable profits, so paying you salary saves the company corporation tax. On the other hand, both you and the company pay Class 1 National Insurance contributions on your pay. You also pay income tax which the company collects along with the National Insurance by operating the PAYE system. However, there is no income tax or National Insurance on pay up to the amount of the income tax personal allowance (£4,745 in 2004–5).

As a shareholder, you may receive dividends from the company. These are a distribution of the profits left after any corporation tax has been paid. There is no National Insurance on dividends. Because the company has already accounted for tax (i.e. corporation tax) on the amount paid out, it comes with a tax credit. If your top rate of income tax is the basic rate or lower, the credit satisfies your tax bill and there is no more tax to pay. (But non-taxpayers cannot reclaim the tax credit.) If you are a higher-rate taxpayer, further tax of 22.5 per cent is due.

You can save large sums in tax by operating as a company rather than as a self-employed person, provided you pay yourself a tax-free salary up to the amount of the personal allowance and the rest in dividends. However, the government changed the rules slightly from April 2004 onwards.

From 1 April 2004, dividends paid to individual shareholders must come out of profits which have been taxed at a rate of at least 19 per cent. So, if you are a small company benefiting from the zero per cent corporation tax band that applies to the first £10,000 of profits, your company will face an extra corporation tax bill if you pay out some or all of those profits as dividends. The rule change does not affect companies with profits of £50,000 or more, since they in any case pay corporation tax at 19 per cent.

Although the rule change means that very small companies may now pay more corporation tax than previously, it is still more tax-efficient to operate your business as a company than as a self-employed person – see Table 7.2. However, you may have good non-tax reasons for choosing self-employment instead.

Table 7.2 Tax on your profits in 2004–5[1]

Profits before wages or dividends	Assuming you take maximum possible profits from the business, tax if you:	
	operate as a company	are self-employed
£10,000	£839	£1,441
£20,000	£2,615	£4,441
£30,000	£4,585	£7,441
£40,000	£6,675	£10,555
£50,000	£10,666	£14,655

[1]Including as appropriate corporation tax, income tax and National Insurance. Assumes the company pays you a salary of £4,745 and the rest in dividends.

Beware of IR35

If your business will involve giving clients your services – for example as a computer consultant, contract engineer, lecturer or nanny – you need to be aware of the so-called 'IR35' rules and how they might affect you.

IR35 applies to companies and partnerships that supply personal services originally to businesses but, since 9 April 2003, also to private individuals. Under the rules, if the Inland Revenue judges that, in the absence of your company or partnership, you would in effect be an employee of the client, you are taxed as if your company or partnership pays you a salary equivalent to the fees from the client. You and your company are liable for income tax and National Insurance in the normal way on this notional salary, wiping out any tax savings you have made by paying yourself in dividends.

Financial aspects of becoming your own boss

Immediate need for money

If you are going to sell your services, you might be able to set up a business with only a relatively small outlay – for example, the cost of a computer, some stationery and advertising. Similarly if you become a home-shopping agent, you should not need to put up any large amounts up-front.

For other types of business or if you are buying a franchise, you are more likely to need a substantial sum of money to get you started. If you are facing an enforced downshift or taking early retirement, you might have a handy lump sum available from your redundancy pay or pension scheme. Otherwise, you might need to borrow or find outside investors. One obvious source is to borrow from a bank. But first check out whether there are any grants available. Your local Business Link★ should be able to help.

Bear in mind that, when raising money from outsiders whether as investors or lenders, it is essential that you have a well-structured business plan (see page 105).

Impact on your income and spending

In the short-term, you could be facing a dip in income while you get your business established and find customers. Your longer-term prospects depend very much on the nature of your business and the amount of time you are prepared to devote to it. Use your business plan (see page 105) to help you estimate the income your business can generate for you.

Impact on your pension

State pension

As a self-employed person, you will be eligible to carry on building up the state basic pension. You do this by paying Class 2 National Insurance contributions. If your profits are low (£4,215 or less in 2004–5), you can opt out of paying these contributions but you will then not be building up state pension after all. Class 2 contributions are very good value (at just £2.05 a week in 2004–5), so be wary of opting out of paying them.

Self-employed people cannot belong to the state additional pension, so you may want to consider paying extra into a personal pension.

If you are a director of your own company, you are an employee. You will be building up both state basic pension and (unless contracted out – see page 223) state additional pension if you are paying National Insurance contributions. However, you can build up both even if you are not paying contributions provided you have earnings at least equal to the lower earnings limit (£4,108 in 2004–5). In 2004–5, it is therefore very tax and benefit efficient to pay yourself a salary of between £4,108 (the level at which benefit entitlement starts) and £4,745 (up to which no income tax or National Insurance contributions are levied).

Occupational pension

As a self-employed person, you have no employer and so cannot belong to an occupational pension scheme. You should make your own personal pension arrangements instead.

If you operate as a company, your company can set up an occupational pension scheme to cover you and any others working for the company. There are special schemes tailored to small companies – get advice from an independent financial adviser★.

Setting up your own occupational scheme has a number of advantages. Contributions to the scheme by you or by the company on your behalf attract tax relief and the amount the company can pay in is effectively unlimited. Moreover, the scheme may be able to lend money to the company and own premises occupied by it.

Personal pension

As a self-employed person, taking out a personal pension (which could be a stakeholder scheme) is the main way open to you to save for retirement. See Chapter 12 for details.

If you run your own company, having a personal pension is a possible alternative to an occupational scheme (see above). Although an occupational scheme has advantages, because of charges it is generally suitable only if you will be putting large amounts into the pension scheme (say, £100,000 or more). If your pension will be smaller scale, a personal pension might be more appropriate.

As a controlling director of your company, you are not eligible to have a personal pension as well as belonging to an occupational scheme. This restriction will cease to apply from April 2006 (see page 239).

Further information

If your business is based on a novel idea, you might be able to patent your invention. To find out more, contact The Patent Office★.

For all matters to do with planning permission, contact your local planning authority★.

Your local authority may offer various grants and concessions to new businesses and can tell you about fairs and markets in the area (that could be a possible sales outlet for your product).

For information about selling by mail order and other distance methods, contact the Direct Marketing Association★. This is a trade body which operates a code of practice for members.

To find business premises, check out the newspaper ads and estate agents local to the area you're interested in.

For help finding appropriate insurance, contact an insurance broker★. The British Insurance Brokers' Association★ can send you a list of its members in your area.

If you are becoming self-employed, let the Inland Revenue★ know. As well as hooking you into the tax system, the Revenue will also send you a useful information pack for new businesses. The Inland Revenue publishes a wide range of free leaflets to help you understand and operate the tax system. Some of those most relevant to self-employed people are listed in Table 7.3 below. For help filling in your tax return, see the *Which? Tax-Saving Guide* published each year by Which?★.

Before starting up as a company, contact Companies House★ for the free leaflets listed in Table 7.3.

Especially if you run a company, but possibly also if you are self-employed, you may need the help of an accountant★ and/or solicitor★. If your main concern is tax matters, choose a member of the Chartered Institute of Taxation★ or the Association of Tax Technicians★.

For guidance on starting up a business, finding out what grants are available, locating suitable training courses, help drawing up a business plan, and so on, try Business Link★ in England, Business Eye★ in Wales, Scottish Enterprise★, Highlands and Islands Enterprise★ or Invest Northern Ireland★.

If you are thinking about working from home, take a look at *The Which? Guide to Working from Home* from Which? Books★.

For general guides covering in detail all aspects of setting up and running a business, check out your local library and good bookshops. See, for example, *Starting Your Own Business* from Which? Books. A comprehensive book is the *Lloyds-TSB Small Business Guide*. The Business Link★ website also has a lot of useful information.

Contact the British Franchise Association (BFA)★ to find out about franchising or whether a particular franchise is a member. The BFA runs seminars and publishes a *Franchisee Information Pack* available from the BFA. It also puts on franchise exhibitions at which you can make contact with a large number of BFA members.

To find out more about becoming a home shopping agent, contact the Direct Selling Association (DSA)★. It publishes a book *Direct selling: from door to door and network marketing*.

For help with pension schemes and plans, contact an independent financial adviser (IFA)★. See Address section for organisations that can send you a list of IFAs in your area.

Table 7.3 Useful free leaflets and booklets

Leaflet/ booklet code	Title	Available from
P/SE/1	*Thinking of working for yourself?*	Inland Revenue*
IR56	*Employed or self-employed? A guide for tax and National Insurance*	Inland Revenue*
IR2003	*Supplying services: how to calculate the deemed payment*	Inland Revenue*
IR222	*How to calculate your taxable profits*	Inland Revenue*
IR227	*Losses*	Inland Revenue*
IR283	*Private residence relief*	Inland Revenue*
NE1	*First steps as an employer*	Inland Revenue*
NE3	*New and small employers – support with your payroll*	Inland Revenue*
IR78	*Personal pensions*	Inland Revenue*
GBF1	*Company formation*	Companies House*
GBF2	*Company names*	Companies House*
GBF3	*Business names*	Companies House*
	Incorporation starter pack	Companies House*

Chapter 8

Leaving work altogether

This is clearly the most dramatic downshift and feasible only if you are no longer dependent on work for your financial survival. It is most likely to be an option if you are at the stage where you can take early retirement. But it can also be a voluntary choice if you are prepared to live simply.

This type of downshift might be forced upon you if you have to stop work because of illness or redundancy and you are unable to manage or find other work. In the past this was common if you found yourself unemployed at any age beyond, say, your late 40s (see 'Maurice's story' on page 130). Many employers simply did not want to take on older workers who they viewed as inflexible and expensive. The climate is changing. The government now runs a special New Deal programme for the over-50s aimed at getting them back into work or self-employment. Moreover, from 2006, work-related age discrimination is to become illegal – however while changing the law is a good start, changing employers' attitudes might take longer.

The big question mark over leaving work completely is your ability to survive financially. There are two sides to financial security. On the one hand, you may be concerned to have a reasonable income to support a chosen lifestyle (and, in that case, you need also to think carefully about how the value of that income will be maintained in future in the face of inflation). On the other hand, you may be able to strip back your wants and necessities to such an extent that your need for money is minimal. But, even if you are drawn to self-sufficiency, it is virtually impossible to exist in current UK society without some hard cash.

Nick's story

Nick retired 4½ years early at age 55. He had been commuting to central London for 23 years and was increasingly frustrated with office politics, poor management and a policy of below-inflation pay rises. He realised he had the opportunity to escape because he had recently separated, his children were now financially independent and, with 31 years in better-than-average pension schemes, early retirement was financially feasible.

'I realised that I didn't want to be rich. I just wanted to have enough money to spend my time doing the things I wanted to do regardless of whether they earned me money or not. And if I could spend the remaining 4½ years doing what I chose instead of working, hopefully I would age less and have a chance of a longer life beyond age 60.'

For 30 years, Nick had wanted to have a go at making and restoring musical instruments. He is now a student at a college in the Midlands learning to do just that. But the transition did not take place overnight. Nick embarked on an intensive seven-month period of planning and preparation. *'There was a huge amount to consider, decide and organise. I'd belonged to three pension schemes and had to find out exactly what I would get from each, including what annual increases they would give, and work out what I'd lose by retiring early. I had to negotiate with my employer about giving me a contract for a few weeks' work each year to top up my reduced pension. I applied to the college and found out about payment of fees. I had to sell my house and find one in the Midlands (where I could buy a larger house with only a small mortgage). I did detailed monthly budgets to check whether I'd have enough money.'*

Probably the most complicated part of the process was sorting out what pensions he would get. *'It took a long time to sort out the pension from additional voluntary contributions that I had made... part of the problem is that you don't get regular statements from the insurance company running the scheme and the company's record was different from my employer's.'*

Early retirement means some reduction in the pension you get but Nick reckons people sometimes make too much of this: *'I think it's sensible to consider the pension you have earned so far (i.e. what you'll get retiring early) separately from the extra pension you'd get by staying on...While the extra will of course be zero if you leave, the pension you have earned so far may be affected very little. In a final salary scheme it will be calculated on fewer years but once it is being paid it will be increased each year. In my case, the pension I'd built up so far was reduced by about 4 per cent a year for leaving early but each year the amount paid is increased by about 3.5 per cent (depending on inflation), so the loss is tiny. From age 60, I'll be getting only 2 per cent less pension from these contributions than if I'd stayed on until 60 (and in the meantime I'll have received 4½ years' pension). The main thing you lose retiring early is the extra pension you'd have built up by staying on.'*

Nick's careful planning seems to have paid off. *'It all turned out at least as well as I'd hoped. I sold my home fairly quickly and arranged to move out just as I finished work. I rented a lovely home for the first eight months, then moved into one I'd bought and had been doing up and which I love. I'm really enjoying the course and have made some good friends. And doing a quarterly project for my old firm keeps me in touch with the people I used to work with.'*

Maurice's story

Maurice was reluctant to talk in detail about his downshift but happy to share useful aspects of his experience. He worked all his life, often for very low pay, but was suddenly made redundant at age 53. Despite many loyal years with the firm, his redundancy package was the minimum his employer could legally get away with (just a few thousand pounds – see page 60 for the current statutory amounts) and frankly Maurice was angry at the shabby way he had been treated. He decided he would never allow himself to be exploited in that way again.

For the first time in his life, he found himself claiming state benefits. Strictly speaking, he was available for work and a jobseeker, but at that time the Unemployment Benefit Office (now called Jobcentre Plus Office) held out little hope of work for someone in their 50s. This made it easy for Maurice to fulfil his aim of not working again for a bad employer.

His benefit income (now replaced by a state pension) was not generous, but Maurice had a roof over his head and had never been extravagant. His income now is around £100 a week and Maurice has developed an alternative lifestyle where friends and family exchange jobs and favours for each other, where there is time to mend and restore instead of throwing away, where a day out means cycling the coast path or walking the cliffs, and a good evening means chatting with friends over cups of coffee and listening to music.

The point of Maurice's tale is that you can have a happy, fulfilled life with very little money, but it depends on your temperament and what you personally want out of life.

Choosing the simple life

You might already be the sort of person who can happily live on a very small income, or you might be keen to explore this as a price worth paying for a greater wealth of time.

If your budget is tight, see Chapter 9 for general suggestions on how to cut your day-to-day spending. But opting for the simple life may go beyond mere belt-tightening. Living cheaply may force you to live simply but it does not necessarily imply going down the self-sufficiency or eco-friendly routes. Nevertheless, many people who yearn for a better work–life balance do also empathise with the green movement and certain aspects of an environmentally sound lifestyle can also accord with saving money.

For example, if you have a garden available, you may be able to save on food bills by growing your own crops or, say, keeping hens. It doesn't even have to be your own garden – lots of people these days do not have time to maintain their gardens and elderly people sometimes cannot manage a large plot. They may be very happy to let you grow produce on part of their land in return for keeping the rest of the garden tidy.

Another possibility might be to rent an allotment. These are usually available for a fairly modest charge, so provided you are green fingered, you should still be able to save on your food bills. (And you might be able to trade any surplus produce with friends and neighbours in return for favours – see page 132.) In some areas, there are 'allotment schemes' where you get together with other local people to work a piece of ground. Depending on the aims of the scheme, you might volunteer to help but be able to have some of the produce free or cheaply, or you might have to pay to join but get a share of the produce. Even if you don't fancy getting your hands dirty yourself, it's worth checking if there are allotment schemes in your area because often they sell the produce to the public at lower prices than you would pay in an ordinary shop. Your local authority* should be able to tell you whether there are allotments available in your area (either owned by your local council or privately) and/or any allotment schemes. Parish and town councils must by law consider providing allotments on receipt of a request from six or more local voters.

If you have some cash to hand – for example, a lump sum from a pension scheme or redundancy pay – you might consider buying an eco-friendly fuel system, such as solar energy or wind-power. Government grants are available to help you do this. You need to work out how long it will take to recoup your initial outlay, but investing in this type of equipment now will reduce your fuel bills in future – in fact, you might make some money if you can sell surplus fuel back to the national grid.

It also makes a lot of environmental sense to repair old household items instead of throwing them away and replacing with new ones and to make things out of, say, wood rather than buying plastic items that are hard to recycle when worn out. Similarly, it makes both environmental and health sense to cycle or walk rather than take a car. Most people caught up in the rat race will say that's great in theory but who has the time to repair or make things, who can spare the extra half-hour to walk? By downshifting you may well find you have the time.

If you are seeking the simple life, you might be attracted to alternative housing – for example, living on a boat, in a caravan or as part of a commune. See Chapter 10 for some ideas to follow up.

Community-based living

Many people see consumerism these days as an intrinsic part of a cult of self that is responsible for the decline of our social infrastructure and sense of community. Some aspects of downshifting can be a way of redressing this social fragmentation.

For a start, people who downshift have deliberately claimed back time from their previously hectic work schedules. One of the most common reasons for doing this is to spend more time with friends and family. They may also be prepared to devote some of that time to voluntary work, such as helping to run local clubs, serving on their local council, getting involved with local festivals or drama groups, and all the other activities that contribute to the 'social glue' of communities.

Downshifters, especially those who have turned their back on work altogether, may be more prepared than others to trade favours. You dig my garden and I'll cook you a meal; you fix my leaking tap and I'll sew you some curtains, you mend my car and I'll give you lifts, and so on. A side-effect of this system is the re-establishing of plenty of human contact. It tackles loneliness, it provides help on hand for niggly jobs that the elderly especially find hard, such as changing a light bulb, and it makes it more likely that someone will notice and help if you have an accident or you are having problems coping.

Living without money

Barter

Another advantage of trading favours is that you can get things you need without using money. And in return you give your services, normally without any tax to pay on the favour you receive in return or any impact on state benefits you might be claiming. (In theory, tax could be due on barter trades, but only if your trading was so regular that it amounted to a business and you were making a profit from the deals.)

However, as with any simple barter system, trading favours has a drawback: there has to be a 'coincidence of wants' – in other words, someone has to want what you have to offer and you have to want whatever they are offering in exchange. You may be happy for me to mow your lawn but I might be reluctant to eat your cooking! Local exchange trading schemes (LETS) aim to get round this problem but have tax and benefit implications.

Local exchange trading schemes (LETS)

How LETS work

These are schemes where members trade favours – usually services and skills, but also goods. However, instead of swapping favours directly, members earn units for their favours in whatever currency the scheme has decided to adopt. The units in a LETS scheme are in effect money, though money with only a restricted range of uses. Unlike ordinary cash, you can't go out and spend your units on just anything. The units can be used only to buy favours from other members of the scheme.

LETS started in a small, informal way but over the last 15 years or so have mushroomed. A typical scheme might work like this:

- members have something in common – for example, they live or work in the same geographical area or belong to the same organisation
- you pay a small annual fee to join which covers the costs of running the scheme. The fee may be at least partly in real money
- you start with a balance of zero units
- you add units to your balance when you do favours for other members of the scheme

- payment for a favour might be partly in units and partly cash. For example, if you were decorating a room for someone, you might get cash to cover the cost of the paint (since you will have to go out and buy that with real money) but units for the value of your labour
- your balance falls as units are deducted when someone else does favours for you
- you can go overdrawn (called having a 'commitment') which means you have a negative number of units which you work off by doing favours for other members of the scheme in order to earn units
- there is nothing to stop someone leaving the scheme while still having a commitment. This means the whole scheme has lost the value of the favours owed. However, LETS work on the basis of mutual trust and members are likely to know each other, so defaults tend to be rare
- one or more people administer the scheme, keeping a register of members, the services they can offer, and their balances.

The units can be organised in different ways. In some schemes, the units have a value in cash, so what is paid for the favour done is essentially its cash value. In some other schemes, units have a time value, so that regardless of the type of favour, the units are based on the time spent. Other schemes have a set value – say, five units – per favour, again regardless of type.

Squids, Beets and Biscuits

In Bristol LETS were first started in 1991. There are now five Bristol schemes and, in addition, they work closely with two schemes based in Gloucester. Together, they have hundreds of members.

The units used by the different schemes are variously Thanks, Totts, Squids, Beets, Biscuits, Acorns and Yatelets. The units in all the schemes represent a given amount of time and can be trans-ferred from one scheme to buy favours from another (a process called 'inter-trading').

Each scheme publishes a directory of the favours on offer from members. These include teaching trumpet, filling in tax returns, weeding, waiting in for the gasman, French conversation, bee-keeping, putting up a shelf and lending tools.

Tax and LETS

You might imagine that LETS could be cunning systems for avoiding tax, but this is not so. The Inland Revenue views LETS in the same way as any other activity. If there is a commercial element, then tax is due. If not, no tax is due.

If you are genuinely just doing favours for other members of the scheme with no element of profit, there should not be any tax due nor any need for you to declare your LETS activity to the Inland Revenue. However, if you are providing services through the LETS as part of your business, tax will be due on the resulting profits. Even if you do not consider yourself to be in business as such, if you are trading through a LETS on what amounts to a commercial basis, tax will be due from you as if you are self-employed (see page 115). It is up to you – not the LETS – to decide whether this is the case and, if so, to declare your self-employment earnings to the Inland Revenue (see Chapter 11).

For favours through LETS schemes, you can charge a mixture of cash and units. If you will have to pay tax, it makes sense to charge partly in cash, since the Inland Revenue will accept only that and not payment in units.

To work out the tax due, you will have to put a cash equivalent value on your earnings in units – you may need to negotiate over this with your tax office.

Deciding whether or not your LETS activity amounts to commercial trading is not clear cut. Turnover is not a definitive factor, but will certainly be looked at as a guide. So, infrequent and isolated trades are unlikely to amount to a business. But regular trading, either in your normal line of work if you are working or in some other unconnected line, may well be judged commercial and so be taxable.

Don't be tempted to cheat the taxman. Be aware that individual LETS are well publicised, so known to the authorities, and the Inland Revenue has the right to inspect LETS records. There are severe penalties if you do not declare taxable profits you make – see 'The black economy' overleaf – and these could affect the people for whom you are doing favours as well as yourself.

State benefits and LETS

If you are claiming jobseekers' allowance (see page 212), to be eligible you must be available for work. If you are trading through a

LETS so extensively that this amounts to a business, the Department for Work and Pensions (DWP) might withdraw your benefit on the basis that you are not in reality available for work at all.

Many other state benefits are means-tested (see page 207). Eligibility and the amount you get depend at least in part on your income. The DWP approach is confused and inconsistent from one case to another, but the value of favours you provide through LETS may be counted as part of your income and so cause a reduction or even withdrawal of benefits. However, with most benefits, there is an 'income disregard' – in other words, a small amount of income you can have that is not taken into account for means-testing. The disregard is typically small – but at least £5 a week in 2004–5, and more in some cases, depending on the benefit involved and your circumstances. To avoid benefit problems, LETS organisers usually recommend that you keep the value of the favours you provide within the disregard limit.

The black economy

Everyone – even a child – is required to pay tax if their income exceeds the amount allowed tax-free each year (see Chapter 11). If you deliberately try to evade paying tax – for example, by working for cash in hand – you are breaking the law and face stiff penalties if caught. For example, if you fail to declare income within six months of the end of the tax year in which you earned it, you can be charged a penalty on top of the tax due equal to the amount of unpaid tax. In addition, you will be charged interest and surcharges for the period the tax remains unpaid. There are also penalties for failing to submit a tax return and failing to keep or produce records. In extreme cases, you could also be imprisoned.

In 2001, a new tax offence was introduced of being knowingly involved in tax evasion. The punishment is a fine and/or up to seven years in prison. It catches not only a person who is moonlighting but also, for example, his or her customers, who collude in the evasion by agreeing, say, to pay cash or accept inaccurate receipts.

There are also penalties if you are guilty of benefit fraud which would include knowingly failing to declare income (or savings) that would reduce or eliminate a claim for state benefits. If you are caught, the state will try to recover the benefit overpaid and, in serious cases, will prosecute which could result in fines and/or a prison term.

Financial aspects of leaving work altogether

Impact on your income and spending

Stopping work completely is obviously going to have a major impact on your income. You need to be clear about how much income you will need, where this is going to come from and how far it will stretch. Chapter 9 aims to help you establish this.

If this is to be a permanent downshift, it might be expected to last for many years. Therefore, you cannot afford to ignore the effects of inflation. Table 8.1 shows the buying power of £1,000 today at various times in the future assuming different rates of inflation. The table shows that, even if inflation averages just 1 per cent a year (very low by historical standards), after 20 years your income would buy a fifth less than it does today (because the buying power of £1,000 would have fallen to £820). At higher rates of inflation, the erosion of your income could be quite alarming.

If you don't want to feel your living standards slip year after year, you need to consider how you will protect the buying power of your income from inflation.

One option is simply to save some of your income in the early years to use later on. However, at least part of your income may be protected against inflation anyway.

If you are dependent largely on state benefits, these are increased each year in line with the Retail Prices Index (RPI). The RPI is one of the main measures of inflation published by the government and is based on the prices of a large 'basket' of goods and services. The inflation you personally experience might be different to that recorded by the RPI because you probably buy a different range of goods and services. Nevertheless, if you are receiving state benefits, that part of your income should be largely inflation-proofed.

Once it starts to be paid, an occupational pension if you work in the public sector is nearly always increased fully in line with inflation. This applies, for example, if you work for the National Health Service, local government, as a teacher, for the police, and so on. Outside the public sector, only some of the largest employers fully inflation-proof your occupational pension. More often, with a final salary scheme (see page 228), it will be increased each year in line with the RPI up to a given ceiling – say, 2.5 per cent a year. If you have a pension from a money purchase scheme, it may be left to you to decide whether to inflation-proof or not according to the type of annuity you choose (see page 229).

The return from only a handful of investments is inflation-proofed. Usually, you'll need to invest in a spread of different assets, some of which give you the chance of a return that beats inflation (but also carry the risk that you might lose some of your money) – see page 162.

If you supplement your income by taking in lodgers (see page 164) or renting out a second property, bear in mind that you will need to increase the rent from time to time and make sure the agreement you have with your lodger or tenant allows for this.

Table 8.1   The impact of inflation on the buying power of £1,000

After this many years:	£1,000 will buy only this much assuming yearly inflation averages:						
	1%	2%	3%	4%	6%	8%	10%
5	£951	£906	£863	£822	£747	£681	£621
10	£905	£820	£744	£676	£558	£463	£386
15	£861	£743	£642	£555	£417	£315	£239
20	£820	£673	£554	£456	£312	£215	£149
25	£780	£610	£478	£375	£233	£146	£92
30	£742	£552	£412	£308	£174	£99	£57
35	£706	£500	£355	£253	£130	£68	£36
40	£672	£453	£307	£208	£97	£46	£22

Impact on your pension

For details of how the pension schemes referred to in this section work, see Chapter 12.

State pension

If you stop work before reaching age 60, you will have gaps in your National Insurance record that may reduce the amount of state pension you eventually get (see page 223). At present, men aged 60 to 64 receive National Insurance credits which mean they are still building up state basic pension even if not working.

You cannot build up state additional pension while not working unless you fall into one of these groups:

- carers who are not working and are entitled to child benefit for a child under the age of six
- carers entitled to invalid care allowance because they are looking after someone who is elderly or disabled
- people entitled to long-term incapacity benefit because they are too ill to work, provided they were in the workforce for at least a tenth of their working life.

If you are within one of those groups, you will build up state additional pension as if you had earnings equal to the low earnings threshold (£11,600 a year in 2004–5).

State pensions do not start to be paid until you reach state pension age, which is 65 for men and currently 60 for women (rising to 65 by 2020) – see page 219. So, if you take early retirement, you will have to manage without any state pension at the start but should build it into your budget forecasts from state pension age (unless you plan to defer the pension – see page 226).

Occupational pension

Clearly, if you stop work, you will stop building up any occupational pension.

Chapter 12 (see page 233 onwards) describes how your occupational pension is likely to be reduced if you decide to take early retirement. Occupational schemes are complicated and they work in different ways, so there is no substitute for talking to your own scheme administrators and asking for a projection of the starting pension you will get if you retire early. Also check what your scheme's policy is on increasing pensions once they start to be paid out. Taking early retirement means you may be retired for a very long period, so you need to consider carefully how you will deal with the impact of inflation – see above.

Unless you have worked for the same firm all your life, you may well have a portfolio of occupational pensions from different employers. You need to get in touch with old employers to tell them you want to start your pension and to get a statement showing how much you will get. See 'Further information' below if you are having problems tracing old employers.

You might also have made additional voluntary contributions (AVCs) – see page 232 – to an in-house scheme offered by your employer or to a free-standing (FSAVC) scheme. Except in the case of added-years schemes (where you buy extra years of membership in a defined benefit scheme – see page 228), the AVC or FSAVC scheme will normally be run by an insurance company which should provide a statement showing how much pension you will get.

If you have pensions from several sources, bear in mind that you may not have to start taking them all at the same time. Check the rules of each scheme to see when the pension must be taken and what increases to your pension rights are offered if you delay the start. You will have to start all your pensions by age 75.

Personal pension

You can pay up to £3,600 a year (£2,808 net of tax relief) into personal pensions and stakeholder schemes even if you are not working. So, if you can afford it, you could still continue to build up your retirement savings.

Anyone can pay into your personal pension or stakeholder pension on your behalf – for example, maybe you have a husband, wife or partner who would do this.

If you take early retirement, there are various options for starting a personal and stakeholder pension:

- you can use the whole pension fund straight away to buy one annuity which will provide you with a pension for life. The earlier your retirement, the lower the income (though the sooner you start the annuity the more you stand to receive in total over your remaining life) – see Table 8.2. If you want some protection against inflation, see page 237
- if the schemes allows, you can use part of your pension fund to buy an annuity now, a further part to buy another annuity later, and so on. This is a way of building in increases to your pension income over the years
- if the scheme is arranged this way, your pension savings might be divided into a cluster of small schemes. You can then choose how many of these small schemes to convert to pension at any one time. Again this is a way of building in future increases
- if your savings are high enough (well into six figures), you might consider income drawdown. Instead of buying an annuity, you

take an income within set limits direct from your pension fund and leave the rest invested. This is a relatively high-risk strategy because if investment growth of the remaining fund is not high enough you can end up with less pension over the years than you would have been able to get from an annuity.

With most personal pensions and all stakeholder schemes, you have an 'open market option' which means that you do not have to buy your pension from the same firm with whom you have had your pension scheme, but can take your pension fund to another provider. With stakeholder schemes, you cannot be charged for exercising this option. With personal pensions, at the normal retirement age for the scheme (if there is one), you can usually do this without penalty, but there may be charges if you are exercising the option at an earlier age. In the absence of charges, it is nearly always worth exercising your open market option and shopping around for the best deal. However, if your current provider offers an annuity at a guaranteed rate that is higher than current annuity rates, you might be better staying put.

Lump sums from pension schemes

With both occupational schemes and personal pensions (including stakeholder schemes), at retirement you can usually take part of your pension fund as a tax-free lump sum before turning the rest into pension.

Even if you need as much income as possible, it is usually worth taking the largest lump sum you can (usually a quarter of the fund). This is because the pension you get is taxable, whereas the lump sum is completely tax-free. If you don't take the maximum lump sum, you are losing tax relief.

If you do need income, invest the lump sum to provide it. One of the simplest ways would be to buy a 'purchased life annuity'. Similar to an annuity that you buy with a pension fund, you hand over your lump sum and in return get an income for life. But, unlike the annuities you buy with a pension fund, only part of the income from a purchased life annuity is taxable – the rest counts as piecemeal return of your capital and is tax-free. See Chapter 9 for other ideas on how to invest a lump sum to provide income.

Table 8.2   Using your pension fund to buy an annuity

If you are this age	A level annuity from a sum of £50,000 would provide you with this much income:			
when you retire:	Each year	Men Over your whole life if you live to the average age shown in the brackets	Each year	Women Over your whole life if you live to the average age shown in the brackets
50	£2,845	£79,489 (77.9)	£2,804	£89,279 (81.8)
55	£3,045	£71,771 (78.6)	£2,956	£80,728 (82.3)
60	£3,328	£64,763 (79.5)	£3,172	£72,829 (83.0)
65	£3,726	£58,349 (80.7)	£3,507	£66,002 (83.8)

Source: Annuity rates from Annuity Direct. Rates for level annuity, no guarantee for non-smoker with pension fund of £50,000. Average life expectancy from Government Actuary's Department.

Further information

If you want to explore self-sufficiency and/or a more eco-friendly lifestyle, browse the shelves at your local library or a good book-shop. Table 8.3 lists some of the books available but there are many, many more.

To get tips and gain skills, you could visit an eco-friendly settlement, such as Findhorn★ in Scotland or the Centre for Alternative Technology★ in Wales. These are model communities which have been designed to have a low impact on the environment. They are open to visitors and also run courses.

Check locally. Your nearest community college, adult learning centre and/or healthy living centre might run courses in, for example, growing your own food, carpentry and other skills that might be useful if you are tending towards a self-sufficient lifestyle.

To find out about government grants for solar, wind power and other energy-efficient ways of fuelling your home, contact Clear Skies★.

To find out more about local exchange trading schemes (LETS), contact Letslink UK★. To find out whether any schemes operate in your local area either email Letslink UK or ask at your local library or local community/council office. If you are interested in starting a scheme, *The LETS Info-pack* is available from Letslink UK.

If you have a lump sum to invest, say, to provide income, consider getting help from an independent financial adviser (IFA)★.

To find out about state pensions generally or your own entitlement, contact The Pension Service★.

Contact the pensions administrator★ at work to find out about your current occupational pension. If you have made AVCs to an in-house scheme, you normally get details of the rules, your entitlement, and so on through the pensions administrator for the occupational scheme, but if there are delays contact the pension provider direct – documents about the scheme should say who this is or ask the pensions administrator for contact details.

If you have an FSAVC scheme, a personal pension and/or a stakeholder scheme, contact the pension provider – usually an insurance company. Documents you were given when opening the scheme and statements should contain contact details.

If you are having trouble tracing an old employer with whom you still have a pension or an old personal pension or stakeholder scheme, the Pension Schemes Registry★ may be able to help. Using its service is free.

If you are using your open market option to shop around for the best annuity at retirement, check out current annuity rates through the FSA Comparative Tables★, with personal finance publishers such as Moneyfacts★ and through independent financial advisers (IFAs) who specialise in annuities★.

Table 8.3 A selection of reading if you are attracted to self-sufficiency

Author	Title	Published by (year)
John Seymour et al	*The New Complete Self Sufficiency: The Classic Guide for Realists and Dreamers*	Dorling Kindersley (2003)
Richard Mabey	*Food for Free*	Collins (1999)
Allan Shepherd and Caroline Oakley	*52 Weeks to Change Your World*	Centre for Alternative Technology (2004)
Diana Anthony	*Creative Sustainable Gardening*	Centre for Alternative Technology (2000)
Soil Association	*The Real Good Life: The Soil Association Guide to Self-Sufficiency*	Cassell (October 2004)
Liz Dobbs	*Growing Your Own Vegetables*	Which? Books (2001)

were able to buy a larger house and still fund their downshift. The larger house gives them scope to take in lodgers if they need extra money, though so far they have not had to do that. John has also been taken on as a part-time lab technician at the college. *'This work is associated with the course anyway, so no real stress there and it is some income. My wife's free-time increase has allowed her to restart her home shopping distributorship at hours to suit us so there is income there as well.'*

How do John and Jenny sum up their downshift? *'So far, very good. Less stress, more free time, no middle of the night call outs, much better nightlife, new friends, milder climate (it's less extreme by the sea), less work than the old job, more choice in what is done and when – better quality of life.'*

Part 3

Coping financially

Chapter 9

Financial planning

Cutting back on work will in most cases mean a fall in income but that does not necessarily mean your living standards will suffer, because your expenses may also fall. Especially if your downshift involves changing your main source of money – for example, switching to self-employment or a pension – working out how your income will change can be complicated. Well before you take the plunge, try, as accurately as you can, to forecast the income you expect to have and your likely spending needs. This should help you avoid nasty shocks later on and give you time to plan how you might deal with any shortfall.

> *'I adjust my lifestyle to my income.'*
>
> Patrick
>
> *'Going part-time was definitely a shock for me because I was the main earner in the house. We've had to cut out certain luxuries, if we want certain things now we have to save up for them instead of just going out and buying them, and we are definitely more careful with money.'*
>
> Christine

Forecasting your income and spending

The only way to get to grips with this is to draw up a detailed budget. It's a good idea to do this first for your income and spending now, and then for your expected income and spending *after* the downshift, so that you get a clear picture of the scale and nature of the financial change you may face.

You should repeat the forecasting exercise for later year(s) if you expect a substantial change, for example, a pension payment kicking in or maintenance stopping when children reach a given age. But beware of anticipating changes that are only tentative and might not be realised – for example, a big rise in profits from a new business or a hoped-for inheritance. Plan cautiously so that you have a robust blueprint for survival.

The calculators and notes on the following pages are designed to help you draw up your budget. If your downshift affects just you, fill in the calculators just for yourself. If the downshift affects others as well, fill in the calculators for your whole household, including your joint incomes and joint spending needs.

In the forecast column, put in the amounts that would apply in today's prices – don't increase them to take account of inflation between now and then. But do make allowance for any expected increases over and above inflation.

Fill in the calculators with weekly, monthly or yearly amounts – it doesn't matter which you choose as long as you are consistent throughout. If you opt for weekly, apportion any monthly, quarterly or yearly income or spending and put the weekly equivalent in the calculators. Similarly, if you opt for monthly spending, put in the monthly equivalent of any weekly, quarterly or annual payments.

Income calculator

Source of income		Your income now	Forecast of your income after the downshift
Take-home earnings from your job	a		
Profits after tax from your business	b		
Income from savings and investments	c		
State pension	d		
Other pensions	e		
State benefits	f		
Other income	g		
Any tax and other deductions not already deducted	h		
TOTAL INCOME AVAILABLE	A		
Add together a to g and subtract h			

Take-home earnings from your job (a)

This is the money from your job that you have left to spend after deducting income tax, National Insurance, pension contributions, and any other deductions made through your pay packet.

For the 'income now' column, you'll find the figure on your pay slip if you are filling in the calculator with weekly or monthly figures or your bank statements. If you are putting in annual figures, take the amount from the form P60 that your employer gives you once a year.

Bear in mind that you will probably lose less in deductions after your downshift because, for example:

- income tax will be lower on a smaller income – see Chapter 11 for guidance on tax
- National Insurance will be lower on a smaller income – see Chapter 11
- pension contributions are often set as a percentage of pay, so fall in value as pay falls
- student loan repayments are set at 9 per cent of income over a given threshold (£10,000 a year at present and due to rise to £15,000 a year from 2005) and stop altogether if your income is below the threshold
- you might decide to stop any donations you currently make to charity through a payroll-giving scheme.

Profits after tax from your business (b)

If you run your own business, put here the amount you draw out for your personal use after tax and National Insurance have been

> *'I was lucky in that, although I lived well away from London after the move, I was working for clients at London rates. With the saving on work-related costs and some serendipitous well-paid projects, immediate income was not really a problem. I was aware though that I had stopped saving for a pension and there was no immediate prospect of putting that right – though I did in due course.'*
>
> Jane

stripped out. You should be able to take the figures you need from your accounts.

Again, the deductions will be lower after the downshift if your profits are lower. For guidance on working out tax and National Insurance, see Chapter 11.

Income from savings and investments (c)

In many cases you will receive income with tax already deducted. If you are a basic-rate taxpayer, this leaves you with the correct amount of income after tax to put in the calculator. You can get the figure from statements from the savings or investment provider or from bank statements where the income is paid into your current account.

If you are a higher-rate taxpayer, there is extra tax to pay and you should deduct this before entering the figure in the calculator. This applies also to other taxpayers who receive savings and investment income 'gross' (in other words without any tax deducted). Alternatively, include the extra tax at 'h'.

If you pay tax at the starting rate or you are a non-taxpayer, you may be able to reclaim some or all of the tax or, in the case of a non-taxpayer, depending on the type of income, you might be able to arrange to receive the income gross.

For more detail about the taxation of savings and investments, see Chapter 11.

State pension (d)

If you have already reached state pension age, include the amount of state pension you get, which is shown on the statement you get from The Pension Service shortly before the start of each new benefit year.

If reaching state pension age is part of your downshift planning, include the amount of state pension you expect to get. You can find this figure on a state pension forecast or a combined pension statement from an occupational pension scheme or personal pension plan.

Your state pension is taxable but paid without any tax deducted. If you also get an occupational pension or personal pension or you still have earnings from a job, the deductions from that will usually include the tax, if any, due on your state pension. If not, either deduct tax from the state pension before putting the figure at 'd' on the calculator or include it in amount 'h'.

Chapter 11 has more details about tax. See Chapter 12 for information about the state retirement pension.

Other pensions (e)

If you are already getting a pension from an occupational scheme or personal plan, include the amount you get after tax has been deducted. You can get this either from the pay slips you receive or your bank statements for the account into which the pension is paid.

Bear in mind that the tax deduction may include tax on other income such as your state pension or income from untaxed investments or property. Make sure this tax is accounted for just once in the calculator – either here or under the heading for the particular type of income.

If you are planning to start a pension as part of your downshift plan, you need to carefully consider how much you will get. To get a rough idea, you can use the benefit statements or annual statements that you get from your various pension schemes and plans, but check the scheme or plan rules carefully to see whether any adjustment will be made if you will be starting the pension before the normal age for the scheme or plan.

As your downshift planning becomes firmer, you need to contact each pension scheme and provider to find out precisely how much pension they will pay if you take retirement now. For more information, see Chapter 12.

State benefits (f)

If your downshift is involuntary due, say, to illness or redundancy, you may be eligible for an income from the state through, for example, incapacity benefit, jobseeker's allowance or income support. Similarly, if downshifting means your income will be low, you might qualify for working tax credit.

Some other state benefits are widely payable, for example, child benefit and child tax credit if you are raising a family, so don't forget to include these if you qualify.

See Chapter 11 for details of the main benefits you might be able to claim.

Other income (g)

Include in amount 'g' any income you get from other sources. This might include, for example, maintenance payments from a former husband, wife or partner, income from renting out property, and so on. If the income is taxed, include only the after-tax figure or deduct the tax under 'h' in the calculator. Chapter 11 has details of which types of income are taxable.

Any tax and other deductions not already deducted (h)

Be careful not to include any deductions already taken off under amounts 'a' to 'g'.

Total income available (A)

For each column, add up amounts 'a' to 'g' and subtract amount 'h'. The result, amount 'A', is the income you should have available to meet your spending needs.

Work-related expenses (i)

If your downshift will result in a drop in work-related expenses – for example, because you are switching to working from home or taking a sabbatical – it may be worth separating out what you currently spend on these items so you can see clearly the amount you might save.

Alternatively, work-related expenses can be included in the appropriate amounts in the rest of the calculator with an adjustment where you forecast that they will change as a result of the downshift.

> *'Financially, the surprise was that the part-time salary really made no difference to my standard of living. I was very careful for six months or so until I could see how the new salary was working through. After that, I relaxed. I had the money to buy clothes, books etc. and have holidays and meals out as and when I wanted. It helps never having had extravagant tastes though. I felt, and feel, as well off as before I made the change. Certainly, there is no travelcard to fund and working at home more means fewer bought lunches.'*
>
> Rachel

Spending calculator

Areas of spending	Your spending now	Forecast of your spending after the downshift
Work-related expenses (commuting, business lunches, clothes for work, journals, work-related entertainment, and so on)	i	
Day-to-day living (food, toiletries, cleaning stuff, small household items, non-work clothing, tobacco)	j	
Transport other than work-related (cost of running car, bus and train fares)	k	
Entertainment (newspapers, magazines, cinema, theatre, concerts, exhibitions, meals out)	l	
Holidays	m	
Health-related (dental charges, eye tests and glasses/contact lenses, health insurance premiums)	n	
Mortgage or rent	o	
Council tax	p	
Water charges	q	
Gas, electricity, heating oil	r	
Phone	s	
TV licence, satellite charges, Internet costs (other than phone)	t	
Buildings insurance	u	
Contents insurance	v	
Home repairs and maintenance including window cleaner, paid help in garden, cleaner	w	
Loan repayments (other than mortgage)	x	
Savings and insurance not covered elsewhere	y	
Other spending	z	
TOTAL SPENDING *Add together i to z*	B	

Day-to-day living (j)

Broadly, this is what you spend during weekly shopping trips plus spending on clothes, shoes, and so on. Don't double count here anything already included above under work-related spending (such as clothing specifically for work).

You should be able to get a reasonable idea of your current day-to-day expenses from till receipts, credit card statements, and so on. If not, try keeping a written record for a month of everything you spend.

Transport other than work-related (k)

If you run a car, include all the running costs such as petrol, car tax, insurance and servicing, unless you have already included these as part of amount 'i'. If you are paying for the car with a loan, don't include the repayments here – instead put them under amount 'x'.

Include any sums spent regularly on travel other than commuting to and from work, such as taxis, and bus and train fares. But don't include holiday-related travel costs – they go under 'm' below.

Entertainment (l)

This is the place for all types of spending on entertainment that are not covered elsewhere, including going out, hiring videos, takeaway meals, and so on. Also include spending on hobbies unless you've entered it elsewhere.

Holidays (m)

What you spend on holidays and short breaks both in the UK and abroad.

Health-related (n)

This is a catch-all for prescription charges, dental charges, opticians' bills, and so on. If your income after downshifting is low, you might be eligible for state help with these.

Also include premiums you pay for any health-related insurance to cover, say, private hospital bills. If you currently get such insurance as a perk of your job and that would cease after downshifting, you need to decide whether you want to replace it with your own policy.

Mortgage or rent (o)

If you are buying your own home with a mortgage, keeping up the monthly payments is essential. A mortgage is secured against the home itself, which means that your lender could seize the home and sell it if you don't stick to the payments.

For your current payments, check your mortgage statement or the statements for account from which you pay. If your payments include the cost of, say, buildings insurance, life insurance, and so on, either include these costs here or under the entries further down the calculator, but don't enter them twice.

Your downshift might involve receiving a lump sum – for example, on early retirement or voluntary redundancy – in which case paying off part or all of the mortgage might be an option which would enable you to reduce this area of spending.

You might be able to remortgage, either to reduce your payments or give yourself more flexibility – see Chapter 10 for details.

It is equally crucial to keep up your rent payments in order to avoid eviction. If your income will be low after downshifting, you might qualify for housing benefit.

Whether you have a mortgage or pay rent, if your downshift involves moving, consider whether your payments after the down-shift will be more or less.

Council tax (p)

Check your most recent bill to see how much you currently pay. Be aware that council tax bills tend to rise faster than inflation, so you might need to budget for some increase in future.

If you will be moving, ask the local council for the area to which you are moving for an indication of council tax charges there and compare with the charge for similar band properties in your own area to get an idea of whether you will pay more or less than you do now. If you already have a particular property in mind, the estate agent should be able to find out for you how much the current owners are paying.

If your income will be low after downshifting, you might qualify for council tax benefit (see Chapter 11).

Water charges (q)

This charge is unrelated to income so you will have to pay it whatever your circumstances. If your water usage is on the low side, you might be able to save money by switching to a metered supply – see page 170.

Different water companies levy different charges, so if your downshift involves moving, you may want to check with the company covering the region to which you are moving the amount you are likely to pay.

Gas, electricity, heating oil (r)

If, after downshifting, you will spend more time at home, these bills could increase. But bear in mind that, if you will be switching to working from home, you should be able to claim tax relief on the part of these costs that relate to your business or, in some cases, your work as an employee – see Chapter 11.

Phone (s)

Again, this bill might increase if you spend more time at home after the downshift, though part could be tax-deductible if you will be switching to working from home.

On the other hand, if you use the phone a lot now in relation to your work and these costs are not fully reimbursed, your bill might go down after the downshift.

TV licence, and so on (t)

From 1 April 2004, a colour television licence costs £121 a year (equivalent to £2.33 a week or £10.08 a month). Also include here anything you pay for digital television subscriptions and Internet charges (other than phone costs which will be included under 's' above) for a dial-up service provider or broadband service.

Buildings insurance (u)

Put the premiums you pay here unless you have included them already with your mortgage payments at 'o' above. If you rent, buildings insurance is normally your landlord's responsibility.

Contents insurance (v)

Put your premiums here unless included already with your mortgage or rent at 'o' above.

Home repairs, maintenance and so on (w)

Although each job on your home seems to be a one-off cost, in practice there is usually a steady stream of small payments, so it is worth budgeting to spend a certain amount each year on these costs. If you're unsure how much to allow, tot up what you've spent over the last 12 months and assume you'll spend the same again each year.

Loan repayments other than mortgage (x)

Put here the total repayments (interest and capital) for any loans you have taken out.

Don't include your credit card bill if you pay off in full each month and what you spend is already included in the categories above – for example, under day-to-day living if you use a credit card to pay your supermarket bills. However, if you have an outstanding debt on the card which you roll over from month to month, do include the higher of the minimum repayment or the amount you generally pay off each month, since you will need to budget for this.

If your downshift will release a lump sum – for example, on early retirement – you could use part to pay off outstanding debts, so reducing the amount you spend on this area.

Savings and insurance not covered elsewhere (y)

This is the place for amounts you pay regularly into savings plans and investment arrangements. Also, premiums for insurance not covered elsewhere should be put here – for example, premiums for life cover.

Do not include contributions to an occupational pension scheme or other plan if they have already been netted out of your income under amount 'a'. But do include contributions to any pension plan you have arranged yourself. The figure to enter is the 'net' amount after deducting any tax relief that is given at source – see Chapter 12 for more details.

Other spending (z)

Any spending that has not already been captured above should be entered here.

Total spending (B)

Add together amounts 'i' to 'z' to find amount 'B'.

Surplus/shortfall

	Your spending now	Forecast of your spending after the downshift
TOTAL INCOME AVAILABLE *From Income calculator*	A	
TOTAL SPENDING *From spending calculator*	B	
SURPLUS/ SHORTFALL *Subtract B from A* *If the answer is less than zero,* * you have a shortfall* *If the answer is zero or greater,* * you have a surplus*	C	

Surplus/shortfall (C)

For each column, subtract 'B' (total spending) from 'A' (total income).

If the answer is less than zero, you are or will be spending more than you have coming in. This is not sustainable over the long-term, so you need to think how you can boost your income and/or reduce your spending (see below). If you can't plan away a shortfall in forecast spending, you must seriously question whether your planned downshift is feasible.

If the answer is zero or more, you have surplus income and, assuming your figures in the calculators are realistic, your plans seem to be financially sound – at least in the immediate period following the downshift. You may, however, need to consider the impact on your living standards in later years, particularly after retirement – see Chapter 12.

'My income is less but my outgoings are even lower. I don't have extravagant tastes and I'm careful with money, but I've got plenty of money to do all the things I want to do.'

Nick

Ways to boost your income

Your earnings

Since your aim is to downshift, you will probably be reluctant to boost your income through increasing the hours you work or by taking on another job. However, there might be some mileage in looking at other aspects of your working arrangements. For example, if you are working for yourself, you might be able to increase the amount you do for more profitable clients while cutting back on work for those which are less profitable; alternatively, you might be able to increase the amount you charge.

Savings and investments

If you have savings you've already built up or a lump sum due from, say, early retirement or redundancy, you could use these to provide extra income. Chart 9.1 suggests investments that might be suitable depending on the level of risk you are willing to take.

'Risk' is commonly interpreted as the possibility of losing some or all of your original investment. This is called 'capital risk'. But risk and return go hand in hand. In general, savings and investments that have no or little capital risk produce relatively low returns. The reason you might accept some capital risk is to give yourself the chance of a higher return.

However, capital risk is not the only type of risk. In particular, if your money is not growing, there is inflation risk – the risk that your buying power may be eaten away by rising prices (see Table 9.1). Another hazard is shortfall risk – the possibility that your investments will not produce the level of income or growth you need to meet a specific commitment. Taking some capital risk is a way to reduce these dangers.

Table 9.1 How inflation can eat into bank and building society deposits

Year	Each £10,000 in your account	After tax income from £10,000 assuming 4.5 per cent a year gross interest rate	If inflation averages 2.5 per cent a year:	
			Buying power of money in your account	Buying power of your after tax income
1	£10,000	£360	£10,000	£360
2	£10,000	£360	£9,756	£351
3	£10,000	£360	£9,518	£343
4	£10,000	£360	£9,286	£334
5	£10,000	£360	£9,060	£326
6	£10,000	£360	£8,839	£318
7	£10,000	£360	£8,623	£310
8	£10,000	£360	£8,413	£303
9	£10,000	£360	£8,207	£295
10	£10,000	£360	£8,007	£288

You can manage risk either by choosing the types of savings and investments that have the level of risk with which you feel comfortable or by choosing a mix of investments with different risks that together balance out to the level of risk you are willing to take.

For guidance on how your tax position might influence your choice of investments, see Chapter 12.

If you keep some money in bank and building society accounts, make sure that you are getting the best return from your savings. Check every six months, say, that you are getting the best rates of interest and be prepared to switch accounts if not. (But weigh up the pros and cons of switching carefully – some accounts do not allow switching without penalty.) You'll find tables of the best rates printed in the personal finance pages of newspapers★, in Which? magazine★ and on most personal finance websites★.

If you need your savings and investments to produce an income over a long period of time, be wary of putting all your money into bank and building society accounts and just living off the interest. Over time, even modest rates of inflation will eat into the buying power of both your original investment and the income it produces – see Table 9.1. This means that, although your money in terms of pounds might stay the same, the amount of things you can buy with

Chart 9.1 Investing a lump sum for income

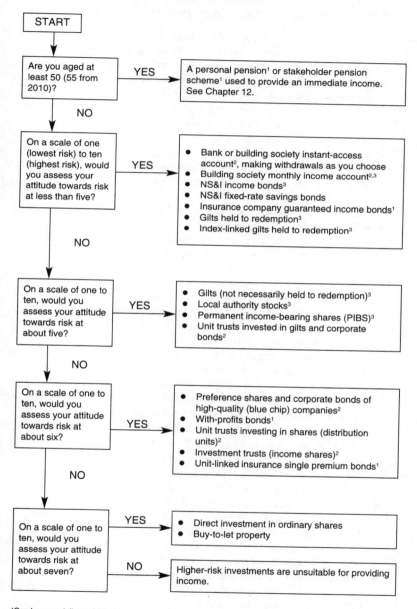

START

Are you aged at least 50 (55 from 2010)? — **YES** → A personal pension[1] or stakeholder pension scheme[1] used to provide an immediate income. See Chapter 12.

NO ↓

On a scale of one (lowest risk) to ten (highest risk), would you assess your attitude towards risk at less than five? — **YES** →
- Bank or building society instant-access account[2], making withdrawals as you choose
- Building society monthly income account[2,3]
- NS&I income bonds[3]
- NS&I fixed-rate savings bonds
- Insurance company guaranteed income bonds[1]
- Gilts held to redemption[3]
- Index-linked gilts held to redemption[3]

NO ↓

On a scale of one to ten, would you assess your attitude towards risk at about five? — **YES** →
- Gilts (not necessarily held to redemption)[3]
- Local authority stocks[3]
- Permanent income-bearing shares (PIBS)[3]
- Unit trusts invested in gilts and corporate bonds[2]

NO ↓

On a scale of one to ten, would you assess your attitude towards risk at about six? — **YES** →
- Preference shares and corporate bonds of high-quality (blue chip) companies[2]
- With-profits bonds[1]
- Unit trusts investing in shares (distribution units)[2]
- Investment trusts (income shares)[2]
- Unit-linked insurance single premium bonds[1]

NO ↓

On a scale of one to ten, would you assess your attitude towards risk at about seven? — **YES** →
- Direct investment in ordinary shares
- Buy-to-let property

NO → Higher-risk investments are unsuitable for providing income.

[1] Can be especially useful for higher-rate taxpayers
[2] Can be especially useful for higher-rate taxpayers if held through an individual savings account (ISA)
[3] Can be especially useful for non-taxpayers because income is or can be paid without tax deducted

Brief outline of investments mentioned in Chart 9.1

- **Personal pension or stakeholder scheme** Tax-efficient ways to provide retirement income currently payable from age 50 at the earliest, rising to 55 by 2010. See Chapter 12 for details.
- **Bank or building society instant-access account and monthly income account** Virtually no risk of losing your capital. You earn interest which is normally taxed at the savings rate before being credited or paid out but non-taxpayers can arrange to receive interest without tax deducted – see Chapter 11.
- **NS&I income bonds** No risk of losing your capital because backed by the government. You earn interest paid out as income with no tax deducted.
- **NS&I fixed-rate savings bonds** No risk of losing your capital because backed by the government. There is the option to have interest paid out as income. Tax at the savings rate already deducted.
- **Gilts** Bonds (basically loans to the issuer) issued by the government. If you hold until redemption (repayment), you know exactly what return you'll get (though this might include loss of some capital). Can be sold before then on stock market in which case return cannot be predicted in advance. These pay out interest at a fixed rate – some gilts provide a relatively high income. The norm is for interest to be paid without tax deducted, though you can opt for deduction of tax at savings rate. With index-linked gilts, both interest and payment at redemption increase in line with inflation.
- **Local authority stocks** Similar to gilts but issued by local authorities.
- **Permanent income-bearing shares** Bonds issued by building societies. They have no redemption date but can be sold on the stock market – this means the overall return cannot be predicted in advance. These pay interest without any tax deducted.
- **Corporate bonds** Issued by companies. If you hold until redemption, you know exactly what return you'll get (though this might include loss of some capital). These bonds can be sold before then on the stock market, in which case the return cannot be predicted in advance. They pay interest without tax deducted.
- **Preference shares** Issued by companies. Pay dividends with tax at 10 per cent already deducted. The company must pay preference share dividends before those on any other class of share and preference shareholders get any money back before other shareholders if company winds up, so preference shares are less risky than ordinary shares.
- **Unit trusts and OEICS (open-ended investment companies)** Funds made up of wide variety of shares and/or other investments selected by a professional manager. You buy units which give you a slice of the fund and can sell units back to the fund manager. Since prices move

down as well as up and cannot be predicted in advance, there is a risk of losing some or all of your original investment. Many pay out an income. If the fund is invested mainly in shares, income is paid with deduction of tax at 10 per cent. If the fund is invested mainly in gilts and/or bonds, income is paid with deduction of tax at the savings rate.

- **Investment trusts** Funds made up of wide variety of shares and/or other investments selected by a professional manager. You get a slice of the fund by buying shares in the investment trust which is quoted on the stock market and you can also sell on the stock market. Since prices move down as well as up and cannot be predicted in advance, there is a risk of losing some or all of your original investment. Some shares have set redemption dates. Income shares are designed to produce mainly income (rather than growth) and income is paid with tax at 10 per cent deducted.

- **With-profits bonds** Investment-type life insurance where return you get is in the form of bonuses, the level of which depends on the performance of a fund largely invested in shares and bonds. However, the insurance company tries to shield you from the ups and downs of the market by holding back some of the return in good years to top up bonuses in bad years. Can be used to provide income (which can be tax-efficient for higher-rate taxpayers because of special tax rules – see Chapter 11) but this increases the risk that you might not get back all of your original investment when you cash in the bond.

- **Unit-linked insurance single premium bonds** Investment-type life insurance where the return you get is linked directly to the performance of one or more funds invested in shares and/or other investments. These bonds can be used to provide income (which can be tax-efficient for higher-rate taxpayers because of special tax rules – see Chapter 11) but this increases the risk that you might not get back all of your original investment when you cash in the bond.

- **Ordinary shares** Issued by companies. Some (but not all) pay dividends with tax at 10 per cent already deducted. Dividends are not guaranteed to be paid and the amount varies. These are usually sold on the stock market. Since prices move down as well as up and cannot be predicted in advance, there is a risk of losing some or all of your original investment.

- **Buy-to-let property** You buy residential property specifically to rent out. Essentially you are treated as if you are running a business and profits from rents less costs are taxable. Risky because you might not be able to find tenants and costs may rise especially if you have taken out a mortgage to buy or need to make major repairs. You might make a capital gain or loss when you sell the property.

it falls and so your standard of living falls too. Spread your money across a range of different assets, some providing income but some which aim to produce capital growth. For example, you might get income from a mix of building society accounts and bond-based unit trusts and for growth choose a range of share-based unit trusts. Get advice from an independent financial adviser★.

Income from your home

If you have the space, you may be able to boost your income by taking in a lodger or two or letting out a self-contained part of your home.

If you are renting, you'll usually need your landlord's permission before you can take in a lodger. And, if you are buying your own home with a mortgage, your mortgage agreement normally requires you to check first with your lender.

You can receive rents up to £4,250 a year from one or more lodgers tax-free under the Rent-a-Room Scheme. For information about the scheme, see booklet IR87 *Letting and your home (including the Rent-a-Room Scheme etc.)* from the Inland Revenue★.

When you sell a home that you live in as your only or main residence, any gain you make from rising house prices is normally tax-free. However, taking in lodgers or letting out your home could mean part of any gain is taxed after all. The rules are complex, but briefly these are key points to bear in mind:

- there is no problem if you take in just one lodger. Any gain when you sell continues to be completely tax-free
- if you have more than one lodger, you'll be treated as running a business and there could be capital gains tax to pay on any gain deemed to come from the business part of your home (regardless of whether you are using the Rent-a-Room scheme to claim tax-free income)
- similarly, if you let out a self-contained part of your home, there may be tax on any gain on that part
- however, there are various reliefs you can claim when working out the tax due which may reduce the tax bill to zero. In particular, you may be able to claim lettings relief which can exempt up to £40,000 of gain from tax– and everyone has a yearly capital gains tax allowance (£8,200 in the 2004–5 tax year).

If you have a second home, or perhaps a caravan, you could let it out to raise some extra money; see page 193.

Capital gains tax

This tax may be due on the profit you make from selling something at a higher price than you paid. The maximum rate is 40 per cent of the gain after deducting any reliefs and allowances.

If your home has a large garden, you might consider selling part to raise a lump sum which could be invested to provide income. You'll get the best price if the land is suitable for building on. But again you need to watch the capital gains tax position. Broadly, the rules are as follows.

If the plot of land on which your home stands, including the garden, comes to no more than half a hectare (about 1.2 acres), there is no tax on any gain you make from selling part of the garden in its unimproved state. Under current rules, you can even get planning permission to build on the garden and still there will be no tax on any gain from selling it (but see below). If you do anything to develop the land yourself – even just marking off the garden as a separate building plot – there may be capital gains tax to pay.

A report commissioned by the government and published in 2004 has suggested that any increased gain on the sale of land due to acquiring planning permission should in future be taxable. However, at the time of writing, it was not known whether the government would take up this proposal or from when it might apply.

If the plot on which your house stands including the garden is larger than half a hectare, a gain from selling part of the garden will normally be taxable unless you can show that the larger garden is in keeping with your home and required for its 'reasonable enjoyment'. But, this may be tricky to prove, especially since you are proposing to sell part of the garden which in itself tends to suggest it is not required for the enjoyment of the home. However, an acceptable defence against this argument might be that you are selling the garden only because of financial hardship. Another could be where you sell the garden to a family member whose presence would not detract substantially from enjoyment of your home.

If you own your home and you are sitting on a large increase in value since you bought it, the most efficient way to raise money from the home is to sell up and buy a cheaper property. This can be a useful option, especially where downshifting involves moving from southern regions where house prices tend to be high to cheaper areas of the country (see Table 9.2).

Table 9.2   How house prices vary across the country

Region	Standard price
North	£103,314
Yorkshire and Humberside	£97,688
North West	£100,534
East Midlands	£125,546
West Midlands	£135,984
East Anglia	£144,910
Wales	£114,870
South West	£160,899
South East	£199,328
Greater London	£232,421
Northern Ireland	£92,718
Scotland	£84,086
UK	£139,716

Source: HBOS House Price Survey, 2003 4th quarter

> *'We had already paid off the mortgage on the house in which we were living in the South of England. If we were to sell that, or remortgage it, we could raise some funds so finance was not an immediate concern ... It soon became apparent that for about two-thirds of the price of the house down South we could get one twice as big in Blackpool! We settled on a five-bedroom home close to the seafront to the college end of town. We could rent a couple of rooms to fellow students if we needed to get some income.'*
>
> John and Jenny

Ways to cut your spending

Day-to-day living and home-related costs

Quite apart from any saving on work-related expenses, you may find that downshifting leads automatically to a cut in day-to-day living costs. If you are currently working long hours and getting home late, there is a tendency to turn to expensive ready-prepared dishes, takeaways and meals out. With more time, you might cook for yourself which tends to be far more economical.

You may also find that you save money because you are doing jobs yourself, such as gardening, decorating and cleaning, which before the downshift you had delegated to paid help.

Nevertheless, downshifting may require you to cut down if you are to live according to your new means. Below are a few ideas for saving day-to-day costs, but once you turn your mind to it, you'll be surprised at how many more you can come up with.

- Switch to own-brands in supermarkets.
- Choose the fruit and vegetables which are currently in season and where appropriate freeze them for use later in the year.
- For fruit and veg that tend to be expensive – for example, melons, cucumbers and peppers – you may save money by growing your own. But be aware that for some other fresh produce, such as potatoes and carrots, it may be cheaper to buy than to grow.
- Buy dry goods, such as rice and pasta, in bulk since they store well.
- Take advantage of offers, such as buy-one-get-one-free, provided they genuinely save you money. For offers on perishables, like meat, freeze the extra for use later on.
- If bulk buys and special offers are too much for you, shop with a friend and split the special deals between you.
- Avoid expensive versions of essentially cheap goods, such as speciality breads and fancy cakes. If you'd miss them, buy the ingredients instead and make your own.
- Keep an eye out in charity shops and car boot sales for things that would be useful. You'll pay a lot less than always buying new items and this is a good way to support recycling.
- Trade informally with friends and family. For example, you might dig their garden in exchange for a share of the crop, or swap your plumbing skills for their needlecraft. See page 133 for more formalised ways to exchange favours.

> '*In the early years, money was tight and I had to do without new clothes and make do. We made very few home improvements. We laugh about how we used to raid the penny jar for money for a loaf of bread some weeks. We both had cars and sold one, so I would walk or take the bus which was hard work with three children but at least I had all day to get there.*'
>
> Lesley

Transport

The main consideration here is likely to be running a car. If you have been a two-car family, after downshifting you might find you can manage perfectly well with just one car.

If you have just one car, weigh up whether you really need it. Just owning a car, regardless of mileage, costs money in car tax and insurance. So, even if you had sometimes to take a taxi or hire a car, you might be quids in if you sold or scrapped your own.

If you are buying a car, bear in mind that you can pay a lot less in fuel, car tax (see Table 9.3) and insurance if you opt for something small and fuel-efficient. And think twice about buying new – a car that's a couple of years old costs a lot less and may be just as reliable.

Table 9.3 Rates of vehicle excise duty (car tax)

Cars registered before 1 March 2001

Engine capacity	Yearly rate of duty
Up to 1,549 cc	£110
1,550 cc and above	£165

Cars registered on or after 1 March 2001

Carbon dioxide emission figure (Grams per kilometre)	Yearly rate of duty		
	Diesel	Petrol	Alternative fuel
Up to 100	£75	£65	£55
101 to 120	£85	£75	£65
121 to 150	£115	£105	£95
151 to 165	£135	£125	£115
166 to 185	£155	£145	£135
186 and over	£165	£160	£155

Source: DVLA, rates for 2004

When you are out on the road, both the AA★ and the government's Doing Your Bit★ website have a variety of tips for cutting motoring costs. These include the following.

- Make sure your tyres are correctly inflated. Fuel consumption can rise by 1 per cent for every six pounds per square inch the tyres are under-inflated.
- A quarter of all car journeys are less than two miles long. Consider walking or cycling instead – as well as saving money, you'll be doing your health good.
- Be choosy when you buy fuel. Especially, fill up before you get on to a motorway – motorway service stations usually charge higher prices than other filling stations. The AA website★ has a free 'petrolbuster' service on its website that helps you find the cheapest fuel outlet in your postcode area.
- Pack roof-racks efficiently and remove them when not in use. The way you pack a roof-rack can improve fuel economy by 2 per cent.
- You're likely to get the best fuel consumption if you stick to speed limits, avoid racing starts and use the highest appropriate gear. Driving at 80 mph instead of 70 mph can increase your fuel costs by as much as 4p per mile.
- Using the rear screen heater and the air-conditioning as a de-mister increases fuel consumption by up to 3 per cent and 5 per cent, respectively. So turn them off as soon as you can.

Holidays and entertainment

These are non-essential areas of spending and you may need to cut back on them. But, with more time to call your own, you may find you are able to substitute new, cheaper forms of entertainment for the ones you used to choose while in the rat race. For example, you might have more meals at home with friends and be able to substitute satisfying walks for a quick half-hour in the gym, particularly if your downshift involves moving to a more scenic part of the world. Be wary of cancelling a subscription to digital television if the alternative would be that you switched to going out more often.

Explore alternative forms of holiday such as home-swapping or joining a town twinning association where you make visits abroad to the twin town(s) usually very cheaply on condition that you host visitors when they make the return visit.

Water charges

Generally, you have no choice but to pay water charges but, if you live in England and Wales and you currently pay a fixed charge based on the rateable value of your home, you do have the option to switch to a water meter.

With a metered supply, you pay a standing charge and then a charge per unit for the water you use. Different water companies levy different charges, so whether you will save depends in part on the company you are with. It also depends on the amount of water you use and the rateable value of your home. According to the water regulator, Ofwat, the average metered bill for water and sewerage is £209 a year compared with £245 for an unmetered household. If you have access to the Internet visit your water company website, which might include an online calculator that lets you check whether you would save with a meter. Alternatively, try the calculator at www.buy.co.uk.

You can have a meter installed free of charge (though your company can refuse if to fit a meter would be very difficult or costly) and you have at least 12 months within which to change your mind if you want to switch back to an unmetered supply. Homes built from April 1990 onwards are usually fitted with meters as standard in which case you do not have the right to switch to an unmetered supply.

With a metered supply, you can save money if you use less water. Table 9.4 shows the average cost of various water-consuming activities.

Table 9.4 Cost of activities using water

Activity	Average amount of water used (litres)	Cost of water based on 14p per litre	Estimated associated heating/ electricity cost	Estimated total cost of activity
Taking a shower	35	5p	9p	14p
Taking a bath	80	12p	19p	31p
Using a washing machine	65	9p	19p	28p
Watering the garden	540 per hour	78p	n/a	78p
Flushing the toilet	7.5–9.5	1p	n/a	1p
Using a dishwasher	25	4p	15p	19p

Source: Ofwat

The government's Doing Your Bit★ website has a lot of useful tips on saving water, including:

- fix dripping taps. One drip per second uses about 4 litres of water every day
- turn off the tap while brushing your teeth. A running tap uses 10 to 14 litres a minute
- don't wash up under a running tap. After just six mugs, you'll have used the equivalent of a whole bowl full of water (around six litres)
- a full load in a washing machine uses less water than two half loads
- take showers instead of baths. Each week you could save enough water to make 1,000 cups of tea
- a third of the average family's water use is flushed down the toilet. Fit a water-saving device in the cistern. You can get a free device from many water companies or from the Save-a-flush★ campaign
- using a hose to wash your car wastes up to 300 litres of water.

Household bills

You do not have to stick with a particular supplier for fuel bills and switching may save you money. Research by the Office of Gas and Electricity Markets (Ofgem) shows that 35 per cent of gas customers and 36 per cent of electricity customers have made the switch. 90 per cent of them found switching easy and the average saving was £60 a year. To switch supplier:

- choose a new supplier, get in touch and agree a contract
- give your old supplier 28 days' notice that you are switching. Do this by phone (using the phone number on your bill) and confirm with a follow-up letter
- pay any outstanding bills from the old supplier
- on the day of the switch, take a meter reading. Check that the old supplier has used this reading to prepare your final bill and the new supplier has used it to start your new billing period. If there is a discrepancy, send the suppliers your meter reading.

The whole process should take around six weeks. You can get a list of suppliers in your area and a comparison of their prices by phoning

Energywatch★, an independent consumer body, or visiting its website. There are several other energy supplier comparison websites★ that take you step by step through selecting the cheapest supplier. To compare prices, you will need to check how much you are currently paying by looking at your last four quarterly bills.

Information from the Internet

If you do not have access to the Internet, bear in mind that you can use it in most public libraries, some community centres and cybercafés.

You usually save money on your fuel bills if you agree to pay monthly by direct debit.

Another way to save on fuel bills is to use less energy. If you have access to the Internet, visit the Save Energy★ website or the government's Doing Your Bit★ website. Here are some of the tips these sites recommend:

- turning down your thermostat by just 1°C, or using just one hour less heating a day, could cut your heating bills by up to 10 per cent
- close your curtains at dusk to stop heat escaping through the windows
- always turn off lights when you leave a room and cut down on daytime usage by adjusting your curtains or blinds to let in as much light as possible. Lighting accounts for around one-fifth of the average household's electricity bill
- if a particular light is on for four or more hours a day, you'll save money by changing to an energy-saving bulb. These bulbs cost more but last much longer – overall each energy-saving bulb saves you around £5 a year
- take a shower rather than a bath. Since a shower uses less water, you save on the cost of heating the water
- eliminate draughts by, for example, fitting DIY brush or PVC seals around your doors
- installing loft insulation to a depth of at least 6 inches can cut your heating bills by 20 per cent

- fit double glazing – it can halve the amount of heat lost through your windows. As a temporary stop-gap, tape polythene across the windows
- when buying new appliances, choose energy-efficient models
- replacing a boiler that is over 15 years old could cut your fuel bills by 10 to 15 per cent.

Loan repayments (other than mortgage)

If you owe money, make sure you are borrowing in the most cost-effective way. Generally, rolling over a large bill on a credit card is expensive compared with borrowing through, say, a personal loan or overdraft.

However, many credit cards have a low introductory rate on a transferred balance. So another way to keep down the cost of credit card debt is to switch every six months or so to a new card to take advantage of the low transfer rate. Be aware that your monthly repayments will normally be used first to reduce the transferred balance and new spending on the card will be charged at a higher rate. Therefore to maximise the time you can benefit from the low transfer rate, consider having two cards: one used just for your transferred balance and a separate card that you use for new purchases.

You can find best-buy credit card and personal loan details in the personal finance sections of newspapers, in Which?★ and personal finance magazines★ and on numerous personal finance websites★. Moneyfacts★ carries details in its specialist magazine (which may be available in your local reference library) and through its faxback service.

> 'The reduced income has been an expected problem but we had planned for this and arranged our finances so that the only debt we had was our mortgage.'
>
> Harriet

Chapter 10

Housing and mortgages

Your home may help you make your downshift possible but paradoxically it can also be the factor which holds you back. If you own your own home either outright or with only a modest mortgage, it is probably your most valuable asset. If you can release the equity from your home – for example, by trading down or moving to a cheaper part of the country – the lump sum you raise might get you started on your own business, fund you through training, or through suitable investment provide an ongoing income – see Chapter 9, page 166. If moving is not an option and you have a largish mortgage, you will be able to downshift successfully only if you can keep up the payments on your mortgage or pay it off. The first part of this chapter looks at your options.

Similarly, if you rent your home, you must ensure that you can carry on paying for the roof over your head – see page 186.

This chapter also looks at what you can do and the help available if you do run into problems paying your mortgage or rent – see page 186.

You may be able to reduce your housing costs and, if this applies to you, simultaneously address your desire for a simpler life by choosing alternative housing – for example, living on a boat, in a caravan or in a commune – see page 189 for some ideas on how to find out more about these options.

Finally, if you have, or can buy, a second property – or, say, a caravan – which you can let out, page 193 onwards looks briefly at the part this might play in funding a downshift.

> '*It was very hard to adjust to having very little money, especially as the mortgage rate was 13 per cent and we had lost a full-time income.*'
> Lesley

Your mortgage

At the end of 2003, the average UK borrower was paying nearly £3,700 a year (£308 a month) in mortgage payments. Making sure you can either pay off your mortgage or keep up the monthly payments is a major financial consideration when planning your downshift.

A mortgage is a loan secured against your home. 'Secured' means that the lender has the right to sell your home and recover the loan from the sale proceeds if you fail to make the loan payments as agreed in the mortgage contract. So you could lose your home if you don't keep up your mortgage payments.

Paying off your mortgage

If your downshift involves receiving a lump sum – for example, a redundancy payment or tax-free cash from a pension scheme on starting your pension early – or you have some savings tucked away, consider using this money to pay off part or all of your outstanding mortgage. That way, you may be able to cut your monthly expenditure significantly – see Table 10.1.

In general, the rate of interest you pay on a mortgage is higher than the after-tax return you can get from savings. Therefore, provided the savings are not already earmarked for a specific purpose (such as an emergency fund), paying off a mortgage is likely to be a better strategy than saving.

If you live in a home which has increased in value since you bought it, another option might be to sell and move to a cheaper property, either buying outright or with a smaller mortgage.

'I moved from the London commuter belt to the Midlands, where I could buy a larger house with only a small mortgage.'

Nick

Table 10.1 Monthly spending you could save for each £1,000 of mortgage you pay off[1]

If the yearly interest rate is:	And you have a repayment mortgage with following remaining term: (in years)						Or you have an interest-only mortgage (any term)
	5	10	15	20	25	30	
1%	£17.09	£8.76	£5.98	£4.60	£3.77	£3.22	£0.83
2%	£17.51	£9.19	£6.43	£5.06	£4.24	£3.69	£1.67
3%	£17.95	£9.65	£6.90	£5.54	£4.74	£4.21	£2.50
4%	£18.39	£10.11	£7.39	£6.05	£5.27	£4.77	£3.33
5%	£18.84	£10.59	£7.90	£6.59	£5.84	£5.36	£4.17
6%	£19.29	£11.08	£8.43	£7.16	£6.44	£5.99	£5.00
7%	£19.75	£11.59	£8.97	£7.74	£7.06	£6.65	£5.83
8%	£20.22	£12.11	£9.54	£8.35	£7.71	£7.33	£6.67
9%	£20.70	£12.64	£10.13	£8.99	£8.38	£8.04	£7.50
10%	£21.18	£13.18	£10.73	£9.64	£9.08	£8.77	£8.33
11%	£21.67	£13.74	£11.35	£10.31	£9.79	£9.52	£9.17
12%	£22.17	£14.31	£11.98	£11.00	£10.52	£10.28	£10.00

[1]Precise amount is likely to vary from the figures shown because different lenders calculate repayments in slightly different ways.

Example

Ben and Helen bought their home ten years ago for £64,000 with a variable rate repayment mortgage of £57,600. The mortgage now stands at £44,470. The interest rate is currently just under 5 per cent a year and they have another 15 years' payments to make. Table 10.1 shows they are paying around £7.90 a month for each £1,000 of outstanding mortgage – in other words, about £44,470/£1,000 × £7.90 = £351 a month in total. This is the amount they will currently save if they can pay off the mortgage in full. If they could pay off, say, £20,000 of the mortgage, they would save £20,000/£1,000 × £7.90 = £158 a month (leaving them still to meet monthly payments of £351 – £158 = £193).

> '*Running my own business means that I cannot rely on a regular income as an employee might. So reducing or eliminating regular outgoings makes sense (particularly as the children and I became wholly dependent on my income after my partner and I split up). Paying off my mortgage was a high priority – for example, more important than saving for a pension. Initially I had a £40,000 loan but I managed to pay it off completely over a period of about five years. This reduced my spending by around £300 a month – though the saving would be less now that interest rates are lower.*'
>
> Jane

Different types of mortgage

If you are not in a position to pay off your mortgage, think how best you can manage the repayments. You do not have to stick with your current mortgage lender or current type of mortgage and might benefit from switching to a cheaper, more predictable or more flexible deal.

Cheaper deals

The mortgage market in the UK is very competitive, so it pays to shop around when you first take out a mortgage. It is also a good idea to review your mortgage from time to time to see if you are still getting a good deal and, if not, be prepared to switch (see page 181).

Most lenders offer discounted mortgages, where the interest rate you pay is artificially low for the first one to five years. This can be very useful if you need to keep down costs for a relatively short period, so might be a useful option if, say, you are considering a temporary downshift, say, to travel or to spend time with children while they are very young.

Many discounted deals are unlikely to be so suitable if your downshift will be permanent. You need to be sure that you will be able to cope with an increase in your mortgage payments once the discount period ends. At that time, you usually revert to the lender's standard variable rate so there will be a big jump in your monthly repayments. For example, if you take out a 25-year £50,000 mortgage at a discounted rate of 2 per cent for two years, using the figures from Table 10.1 you'd pay around £4.24 × £50,000/£1,000 = £212 a month. But if, at the end of two years, you revert to a standard variable rate of, say, 5 per cent, your payments would jump to about £5.84 × £50,000/£1,000 = £292 a month.

At the end of the discount period, you might be able to shop around for a replacement special deal at a more competitive price than the standard variable rate but, with many (though not all) discounted deals, the lender levies high early redemption charges for several years extending beyond the end of the discount period – called an 'extended tie-in'. This makes switching expensive and effectively locks you into the lender's standard variable rate for a while. But, with some discounted deals, the early redemption penalties apply only during the discount period, leaving you free to switch to a new deal at the end.

Example

Sam has had a discounted rate repayment mortgage on which interest is currently 4 per cent. The mortgage which now stands at £60,000 has another 20 years to run. He could get a new discounted mortgage still at 4 per cent. Table 10.1 (see page 176) shows that his monthly payments would be £6.05 for each £1,000 of mortgage, in other words £50,000/£1,000 × £6.05 = £302.50. Instead, he could take out an all-in-one mortgage. The interest rate he would have to pay is higher at 5 per cent a year but, provided he uses the current and savings accounts that form part of the package, the positive balance in those accounts will be deducted from his mortgage balance before interest is worked out. On average, Sam has a current account balance of £700 and he has savings of £12,300. So his average adjusted mortgage balance would be £50,000 – £700 – £12,300 = £37,000. Using Table 10.1, at 5 per cent a year interest, the monthly payments would be £37,000/£1,000 × £6.59 = £243.83. Previously, he was earning virtually nothing on his current account balance but 3 per cent a year after tax on his savings, so he has given up (£12,300 × 3%)/12 = £30.75 a month interest. So switching to an all-in-one mortgage would save Sam £302.50 – £243.83 – £30.75 = £27.92 a month.

Another possibility for reducing your monthly payments is to opt for an all-in-one mortgage. With these, you not only take out a mortgage with the lender but you also run your current account and often a savings account with them too. These do not earn interest, but the positive balances in your current and savings accounts are deducted from the outstanding balance of your mortgage before the monthly interest charge is worked out. This reduces the cost of your mortgage and is tax-efficient because effectively your savings are earning the mortgage rate and moreover earning this rate tax-free. Such an arrangement is also flexible because savings being used to keep down the cost of your mortgage are still available should you need to use them for something else, which they would not be if you simply used the savings to pay off part of the mortgage outright.

On the downside, the mortgage rate for most all-in-one mortgages tends to be relatively high compared with other mortgage deals.

Predictable payments

In the UK, the norm is generally to choose a mortgage whose interest rate is variable – in other words, changes in line with interest rates in the economy as a whole as they go up and down – see Table 10.2. The disadvantage of variable-rate mortgages is that, when interest rates are rising, your monthly payments may increase significantly. This makes it harder to keep a rein on your spending.

Especially if money is tight it may make sense instead to go for a fixed- or capped-rate mortgage, where your monthly payments are either set at a fixed amount each month or vary but cannot go above a set level. It is possible to take out a mortgage where the interest rate is fixed for as long as 25 years, giving you absolute certainty about your monthly payments throughout the whole of a typical mortgage term. However, such long-term fixes are rare and most people who take out a fixed- or capped-rate mortgage do so just for a few years, often then switching to another fixed- or capped-rate loan for a further set period. If interest rates have risen in the meantime, monthly payments following the switch will be higher than they were before.

As with discounted mortgages (see above), some fixed-rate and capped deals have extended tie-ins, so that you face hefty redemption penalties if you try to switch mortgage in the year or two after the fixed-rate or capped-rate deal has come to an end and reverts to the lender's standard variable rate. But there are many deals which do not have extended tie-ins, so shop around.

Table 10.2 Take-up of different types of mortgage in recent years

Type of mortgage	Percentage of new loans of this type		
	2003	2002	2001
Variable-rate	61%	73%	73%
Fixed-rate	36%	23%	27%
Capped-rate	3%	4%	not available

Source: Survey of Mortgage Lenders (joint survey by Council for Mortgage Lenders and Office of the Deputy Prime Minister)

If you do not opt for a fixed-rate or capped-rate mortgage, you should plan how you will cope with any increase in the mortgage rate you pay. You can use Table 10.1 to work out the approximate increase in your monthly payment for each £1,000 of mortgage that you have if interest rates rise. For example, suppose you have a £50,000 25-year repayment mortgage and the interest rate rises from 5 per cent a year to 6 per cent. Table 10.1 shows that your monthly payments for each £1,000 would rise from around £5.84 a month to £6.44. This means your payments would rise by about (£6.44 – £5.84) × £50,000/£1,000 = £30 a month.

Cost of linked savings

Apart from the type of interest rate you choose, there are two types of mortgage according to the way you repay the original loan. With a repayment mortgage, your monthly payments cover both interest and repayment of the original amount you borrowed (the 'capital'). Provided you meet all the payments, you will have paid off the whole loan by the end of its term.

With an interest-only mortgage, your monthly payments cover only the interest on the loan and the amount you owe stays the same throughout the mortgage term. You have to make some other arrangement to pay off the capital at the end of the mortgage term. Usually you do this by paying monthly into some kind of savings arrangement.

In the past, the most common type of savings arrangement linked to a mortgage was an endowment policy. An endowment policy is a type of investment-type life insurance that builds up a cash-in value. The hope is that the cash-in value will be enough by the end of the mortgage term to pay off the loan. However, there is no guarantee that the policy will produce enough – whether or not it does depends on stock market performance.

Endowment policies are designed to run for the long-term and often produce poor returns if you stop them or cash them in early. This means that, if you decide to switch to a better-value mortgage, you should also consider separately what to do about the endowment policy (see page 183). *Which?* magazine suggests that most people should avoid endowment mortgages because they are risky, expensive and inflexible. If you think you have been mis-sold an endowment policy, *Which?* has a website, *www.endowmentaction.co.uk*, that will help you decide whether to make a complaint.

Flexibility

An alternative approach to managing your mortgage is to opt for a flexible mortgage. With most of these deals, you pay the lender's standard variable rate, so these are not the cheapest loans on the market. However, built into them, they have the flexibility to let you make extra payments as and when you want to and, importantly, to make underpayments and take payment holidays. Flexible mortgages can be a good choice if your income is likely to vary, for example, because of temporary career breaks to care for children or where profits from your own business are volatile.

Different flexible mortgages work in different ways, but often you must have had the mortgage at least six months before you can take a payment holiday or underpay. If you have made overpayments, some of these mortgages let you borrow back part of your overpayments as a cash lump sum.

Switching your mortgage

Which type of mortgage?

Your first step in switching is to decide why you want to make the switch and therefore which type of mortgage will suit you best – see Table 10.3.

Table 10.3 Which type of mortgage should you switch to?

Your goal	Type of mortgage to consider
Save money every month	• Any type; look for a cheaper interest rate than you are currently paying • If you have savings, consider paying off part or all of your mortgage instead or, if the savings are earmarked for other use, consider an all-in-one mortgage
Save money each month for a set period – for example, during a temporary downshift	Discounted mortgage
More certainty over how much you must pay each month	Fixed-rate mortgage or capped-rate mortgage
Freedom to reduce and increase monthly payments, for example, as income fluctuates	Flexible mortgage

Having decided on the type of mortgage, shop around for the best deals – see 'Further information' on page 194. Decide on the mortgage term you're after. Unless you particularly want to extend the term, the new mortgage should normally be designed to last for the same amount of time as remains on the old mortgage. For example, if you originally took out a 25-year mortgage five years ago, look at a 20-year term for the new mortgage.

Extending the mortgage term is a way of reducing your monthly payments, though the total you'll pay over the whole mortgage term will be greater. For example, using the data from Table 10.1, a £50,000 repayment mortgage over 20 years at 5 per cent a year would cost £6.59 × £50,000/£1,000 = £329.50 a month and £329.50 × 12 × 20 = £79,080 over the full 20 years. Borrowing over 25 years instead would reduce the monthly outlay to £5.84 × £50,000/£1,000 = £292 a month but increase the overall cost to £292 × 12 × 25 = £87,600. You should not normally take out a mortgage whose term will extend beyond the age at which you expect to retire because you might then have too small an income out of which to meet the mortgage payments.

Decide whether you want a repayment or interest-only mortgage. For many people, a repayment mortgage will be best because it offers:

- **certainty**. Provided you keep up the payments, the loan is fully paid off by the end of the term
- **no stockmarket risk**. With most interest-only loans, you pay into an investment which you hope will grow by enough to repay the loan at the end of its term. You are gambling that the investment, whose growth is typically linked to the stockmarket, will yield more than the cost of the loan. You avoid this gamble completely if you opt for a repayment mortgage
- **flexibility**. If you do run into problems keeping up your repayment mortgage payments, you may be able to reduce them by extending the mortgage term or waiving the capital repayments for a while. Interest-only mortgages tend not to be so flexible

However, if you already have an endowment mortgage, you might consider taking out another interest-only mortgage and continuing to use the existing endowment policy as the main vehicle for eventually paying off part or all of the new loan. You should certainly be wary of just stopping or cashing in the endowment policy early because it might then give you only a very poor return. If you no longer need the endowment policy, an alternative to stopping it or cashing it in might be to sell the policy on the 'traded endowment policy (TEP) market'. See *Further information* on page 194.

The cost of switching

Next, check out the cost of switching. Your present lender will usually make some change if you pay off your current loan. If you are still within the period of a special deal or your current mortgage has an extended tie-in (see pages 178–9), this charge could be hefty. Otherwise, there might just be a relatively small administrative charge. Ask your existing lender to give you a redemption statement. This will set out the charges together with the amount of your outstanding loan.

There will also be costs involved in taking out the new loan. Typically, you must pay a valuation fee and legal fees, though some lenders will cover or reimburse these costs usually up to a given limit. Where you opt for a special deal (such as a fixed or discounted rate) there may also be an arrangement fee (also called a 'booking fee') of around, say £150 to £500. If you are borrowing more than, say, 75 per cent of the value of your home, you might also have to pay a high lending fee – also called a 'mortgage indemnity guarantee

(MIG)' or 'mortgage indemnity premium (MIP)'. This is an insurance policy that protects the lender (but not you) if you fail to keep up the agreed mortgage payments. If you have used a broker to find your mortgage, there may also be a broker's fee.

Total up the costs to decide whether switching makes financial sense for you.

Example

Sam wants to switch from his current lender to a new lender offering an all-in-one mortgage. He has worked out that, given his outstanding balance of £50,000, the switch will save him around £30 a month (£360 a year). But to judge whether the deal is worthwhile, he must check out what charges are involved. He has had a five-year discounted mortgage with his present lender and the discount period is just coming to an end. There is no early repayment charge. Sam will have to pay a valuation fee (£250) and legal costs (£350). So in total the switch will cost him £600 in order to save £360 a year. It will take him less than two years to recover the cost of switching, so he reckons it is worth going ahead.

Will your existing lender make you an offer?

Before going ahead with the switch, contact your existing lender. Explain the new deal you are intending to switch to and ask your existing lender whether it is willing to offer you something similar in order to keep your custom. If it does, you should save on some costs, such as valuation and legal fees.

Making the switch

Once you've decided to make the switch, you need to complete the lender's application form. The lender will run a credit check and ask you to supply various documents (for example, to prove your identity and your earnings). If all goes well, the lender will then make you an offer. Provided you are happy with the offer, sign it and appoint your solicitor or conveyancer to proceed with the transfer. A completion date will be set by which time you sign the mortgage deed. The new lender then releases funds to your solicitor or conveyancer who passes these on to the old lender to repay your existing mortgage. (If you have increased the amount you are borrowing beyond the amount outstanding on the original mortgage, the solicitor or conveyancer releases the remaining funds to you soon after completion.)

Mortgage payment protection insurance

You can take out insurance either at the time you start a mortgage or later on which is designed to take over paying your mortgage interest (but not any capital repayments) if you are unable to work because of illness or unemployment.

On the face of it, this type of insurance is a good idea. If as a result of illness or unemployment your income is very low (and you have little in savings to fall back on), you might qualify for state benefits to help towards your mortgage payments (see page 210) but this help does not normally kick in until the tenth month of your claim. Mortgage payment protection insurance can be useful to fill that gap (and in practice normally pays out for a period of one or sometimes two years).

However, as with any insurance, you need to check what conditions and exclusions apply. In particular, such policies do not normally pay out if you have to stop work because of a health problem which you already had at the time you took out the policy (called a 'pre-existing condition'). Also check carefully to see whether the policy will pay out in the event of unemployment given your particular circumstances: some policies do not cover casual workers; part-timers may need to work at least 16 hours a week to be eligible; if full-time, you may need to have been employed at least six months before you can claim; there may be special conditions if you are self-employed or on a fixed-term contract.

Even where the cover offered is appropriate, you might feel mortgage payment protection is not necessary for you if, say, you already have income protection insurance (that would replace a substantial part of your income in the event of illness) or a good sick-pay scheme through your job, you have savings which could be used to meet the mortgage payments for a reasonable period, your mortgage is only small, and/or you have a flexible mortgage (see page 181) that would allow you to take a payment holiday or reduce the monthly payments for a while.

Renting your home

If you live in rented accommodation, you could be evicted if you don't keep up to date with the rent. Therefore, you need to ensure that after the downshift you will have enough money to cover this key area of spending.

Your rights

If you rent your home, you will usually have signed a tenancy agreement which is a contract giving you the right to live in a property in return for paying rent. The contract exists even if it is not written down. But obviously it is harder to prove what was agreed if there is only an oral contract, so you should always ask for a written statement of the contract terms. In Scotland (but not the rest of Britain), you have the legal right to insist on a written contract. If your landlord refuses, you can take the matter to the Sheriff Court★.

There are different sorts of tenancy contract but, if you are renting privately, you are most likely to have an assured shorthold tenancy. This must last for a minimum period of at least six months and the landlord has the right to ask you to leave after the first six months. At the end of each period, unless the landlord has given you notice to quit, you have the right to renew the tenancy. The landlord must normally give you two months' notice if he or she wants you to leave.

If you are a council tenant, after an initial period (usually lasting a year) you will normally have a secure tenancy. There is no limit to the period of your tenancy under this type of agreement.

All sorts of terms can be written into a tenancy agreement, but if they are too one-sided and give your landlord an unfair advantage, you may be able to challenge the terms under the Unfair Terms in Consumer Contracts Regulations 1999. Get advice before going down this route (see page 194).

Your rent

You must pay rent, usually in advance, at the intervals agreed under the contract. This could be, say, weekly or monthly. It is crucial to keep a record to prove that the rent has been paid just in case there is any dispute. If you pay weekly, your landlord is required to provide you with a rent book where the date and amount paid is logged and signed by you both. You might arrange to pay, say, monthly by direct debit or standing order straight from your bank account. In this case you'll have a record in your bank statements of what was paid and when.

Your landlord usually has the right to increase the rent, but only after following a set procedure. This varies depending on the type of tenancy agreement that you have. For example, with an assured shorthold tenancy, the landlord can normally increase the rent at the end of a tenancy period. If you do not want to pay the higher amount, you do not have to renew the tenancy.

Rent for council and housing association properties is usually lower than rent for equivalent private rented accommodation.

If you fall behind paying your rent, your landlord can apply for a court order to evict you and force you to pay the rent that you owe. Therefore it is essential that, when planning any downshift, you consider how you will keep up the rent payments.

If your income and savings are low, you may be eligible for housing benefit which is a state benefit designed to cover part or all of your rent (see page 210).

Other people's rent

If you are sharing a property with other people, the contract could be drawn up in several ways:

- between the landlord and just one of you. The person named in the agreement is the only one legally responsible for paying all the rent, although you will probably arrange privately to share the rent between you
- between the landlord and all of you. You will all collectively be responsible for the rent, so if one person does not pay their share, the others have to make up the shortfall
- between the landlord and each one of you. This is usually the best arrangement in that you are not responsible if one of the other tenants fails to pay their share of the rent.

What to do if you can't keep up your mortgage or rent

Mortgage and rent payments are both priority debts. A 'priority debt' is one where the consequences of not paying what you owe are severe and therefore it is in your interests to do all you can to meet the payments. With your mortgage or rent, if you don't keep up the payments you could lose your home.

Debt problems have a nasty habit of getting worse if you ignore them, so the crucial first step is to admit as soon as possible that you have a problem. Next, think about how you might resolve the problem. Work out a budget showing your income and what you spend – see Chapter 9 for guidance on how to do this. Work out how much you can afford each week or month to pay off your debts if you cut out unnecessary spending or take steps to increase your income. Make sure you are claiming any state benefits for which you are eligible – see Chapter 11.

Your mortgage or rent might be just one of several debts that you are struggling to manage. Sort the debts into priority debts – see Table 10.4 – and the rest, for example, credit cards, overdraft, unsecured personal loan (called non-priority debts). The worst that can happen with non-priority debts is that a court can order you to pay them off bit by bit according to what you are judged to be able to afford.

Concentrate on paying off priority debts first. With your mortgage, try to pay the interest in full. Don't worry about any capital repayments – your lender can probably be persuaded to suspend those at least for the time being. With rent, try to cover your current rent in full plus a bit extra to gradually reduce the backlog you owe. Any income left over can be put towards clearing the non-priority debts bit by bit.

Having worked out your plan, contact your creditors straight away. Explain the problem and how you intend to pay off your debt. It's best to do this in writing so that you have a record of what you agree and to guard yourself against being exposed to pressure to agree to higher payments than you can really afford. If you do get in touch by phone or in person, make notes of what is said and agreed.

There are lots of organisations that can help you work through the procedure outlined above – see 'Further information' on page 194.

Table 10.4   Priority debts

Type of debt problem	What can happen
You fail to pay rent	You could be evicted
You don't keep up mortgage payments	The lender can take your home away from you
You don't keep up payments for other loans secured on your home	The lender can take your home away from you
You don't pay your fuel bills	Your gas or electricity can be cut off
You don't pay your phone bill	The phone can be cut off. (Not a priority dent if you could manage without a phone)
You don't pay your TV licence	You can be fined and/or sent to jail and your possessions can be seized to pay the arrears and fines
You don't pay your council tax	You can be fined and/or sent to jail and your possessions can be seized to pay the arrears and fines
You don't pay other taxes	You can be fined, your possessions can be seized to pay the arrears and fines; you could be declared bankrupt
You don't pay Magistrates' Court fines	You can be sent to jail and/or your possessions can be seized to pay the arrears
You don't keep up hire purchase payments (e.g. for a car)	The lender can take back the goods. (Only a priority debt if the goods are essential to you – e.g. you need the car to get to work)

Alternative housing

Caravans

Living in a caravan can be attractive both as a form of cheap housing and as a way of getting back to nature. You could opt for a permanently sited home or the life of a traveller.

It's estimated that about a million people live in mobile homes on permanent residential sites. Typically these are bungalow-style homes that are very different from the type of caravan you tow behind a car. They are often situated in attractive parkland and so are sometime referred to as 'park homes'. Normally, you buy the home but not the land on which it stands.

Residents of static mobile homes are protected in law by the Mobile Homes Act 1983 which sets out your rights, among other matters, to the following:

- **a written agreement** with the site owner. This must be provided within six months. Some terms must be included by law, others are subject to negotiation between you and the site owner. You can apply to court or an arbitrator to alter some terms of the agreement
- **security of tenure**. Usually you have the right to live in your home indefinitely. You can end your agreement with the site owner if you give four weeks' notice. But the site owner can end the agreement only with permission from a court or arbitrator and even then only if any of the following three grounds apply: you are not living in the home as your main residence; the home because of its age and condition is detrimental to the site or will be within the next five years; or you have broken the terms of the agreement

In general, you buy the home as situated on a particular site. The site owner cannot move your home to another pitch unless the agreement says that is allowed or you agree to the move. You have the right to sell your home, or to give it to a member of your family, in which case your agreement with the site owner passes to the new mobile home owner(s). The owner has the right to approve the new home owner(s) but may not withhold his or her approval unreasonably.

A permanently sited mobile home is generally cheaper than an ordinary house but can still cost you, say, £60,000 or £100,000. The newer the home, the more expensive it is likely to be. This form of home tends to depreciate (lose value) with age but prices do also tend to move up and down with ordinary house prices. So any house price inflation might offset or even outweigh the loss in value due to age.

You pay a pitch fee – say weekly or monthly – for the site your home occupies. You also pay for services provided by the site owner.

If you travel around in your caravan, the Mobile Homes Act does not apply. Bear in mind you do not have the right to stop just anywhere. You should use proper sites or have permission from the landowner. Consider joining the Camping and Caravanning Club★ so you can use its sites.

All privately owned caravan sites – whether for permanent residential use or touring caravans – must be licensed by the local authority. If you have problems which the site owner refuses to sort out, you could complain to the local authority★.

Boats

The Residential Boat Owners' Association (RBOA)★ estimates that about 15,000 people live on boats in Great Britain, on canals, rivers and coastal moorings. There is no single lifestyle that sums up boat living: you could moor in a rural area or in a town. You could adopt a nomadic existence, cruising continuously, or you could have a permanent mooring. You could have a fairly basic home or a boat with all the luxuries of a land-based flat. The type of boat you choose will depend on the type of lifestyle you want.

If moving on to a boat is part of your downshift plan, cost is likely to be an important consideration. These are the main costs:

- **buying a boat**. The sky is the limit when it comes to boating. If you want to cruise the West Indies in a luxury yacht, you are talking hundreds of thousands of pounds, but if you'll settle for a narrow boat on a British canal, you could buy second hand for less than £20,000

- **arranging a mooring**. If you intend to moor for any length of time, you will need to hire or buy a mooring. Hiring starts at around £800 a year in a rural area but is much higher (say, £2,500) for a popular London location, like Little Venice. There is a waiting list for moorings in some areas, especially London and the south-east, so you can't be sure of living where you would ideally like. Some boats are sold complete with a mooring. If you opt for continuous cruising (defined as never staying in one place for more than 14 days), you will have to pay for moorings as you go (cost will vary but, say, around £6 a night)

- **getting a navigation licence**. Most of Britain's canals, rivers, estuaries and harbours fall under the jurisdiction of British Waterways★ or the Environment Agency★, from whom you will need an annual navigation licence. The cost varies depending on the waterways for which you wish to be covered and the size of boat you have, but you might pay around, say, £500

- **Boat Safety Scheme certificate**. This is basically equivalent to an MOT for a car and you need an inspection once every four years. The inspection must be carried out by an approved examiner. For most boats, production of a valid certificate is required in order to obtain your navigation licence

- **buying insurance**. Most navigation authorities insist that you have at least third-party insurance (to cover injury or damage you cause to other people or their property). It usually makes sense to pay extra for comprehensive cover to pay out for damage to or loss of your own boat.

In addition, you will have the costs of heating your boat, paying for electricity (moorings typically include a hook-up to a metered supply), fuel if you will be cruising, and so on.

Detailed homework is essential before taking the plunge – see 'Further information' on page 195 for sources to follow up.

Communes

Communes come in all shapes and sizes. The essential feature is that at least some of your daily living is shared with others. This could range simply from some communal meals right through to working the land together.

The way communes are financed varies. If you join an existing commune occupying a formal building, you may have to buy a share of the home – raising a mortgage if necessary to do so. When you leave, your share is sold to an incoming new member whose lump sum payment is then given to you. In many communes, you pay a regular maintenance fee that covers, say, food, heat, light and so on. If there was no lump sum to pay on joining, the maintenance fee might be set higher to cover mortgage repayments as well. Other communes have no or only a small maintenance fee but you work for the community for no pay. In yet others, you carry on with your work outside the commune and contribute a percentage of your income.

Often life is simple and traditional skills, such as carpentry, baking, building and pottery are valued. Living in a commune may be a chance to learn new skills like these.

Existing communities will not necessarily have vacancies and, even where they do, you and the commune might not be suited. It is essential that you visit the commune and get to know how it works, the people there, its aims and ethos so that both you and the commune can judge whether you will fit in.

Letting out a second property

You might be attracted to the idea of funding your downshift at least in part by rental income from letting out a second property or even a string of different properties. 'Buy-to-let' has become very popular in recent years because the boom in property prices has meant that, in addition to the potential for rental income, you might also make a substantial capital gain when you eventually sell the property.

However, buy-to-let is no easy route to making money, especially if you need a mortgage in order to buy the rental property. Points you should consider include the following:

- **how much you can borrow** Usually the maximum buy-to-let mortgage you can have is 80 per cent of the value of the property – so you'll need to find a fifth of the price yourself (and more if the valuation is lower than the purchase price). The loan may also be restricted depending on the amount of rental income the property is expected to generate

- **type of mortgage** You have the usual range of mortgages to choose from – see page 177. If you intend to sell the property eventually to pay off the loan, an interest-only mortgage could be appropriate which would keep down the monthly cost. Consider a fixed-rate loan or, if not, make sure that you will be able to manage any increase in interest rates

- **the need to choose your property carefully** You need to buy a property that will be easy to let – for example, in a pleasant, safe neighbourhood, close to shops, school, college. You may need to spend quite a bit of money bringing the property up to scratch – fitting a good kitchen and bathroom, smart decoration, and so on. Bear in mind that you will not be earning any income during periods the property stands empty but you will probably still have costs, such as the mortgage payments, to meet

- **the need to choose tenants carefully** You or someone else needs to vet would-be tenants and follow up references. You might want to hand this job to a letting agency, but of course you will then have agency fees to pay

- **maintaining the property** There will be ongoing costs for regular maintenance and from time to time for repairs. Can you do the work yourself, will you have to hire decorators, builders and so on? Can you organise the work yourself or will you want to delegate this to an agency (which will, of course, charge a fee)

- **tax on rental income** You are basically treated as if you are running a business which covers all the properties you rent out. You can claim tax relief for expenses you incur, including interest on a mortgage to buy the rental property (even if the mortgage is secured, say, on your own home rather than the rental property). However, there are some differences between the taxation of rental income and the taxation of normal business profits. The Inland Revenue★ publishes a booklet explaining the position – see *Further information* below

- **taxation of any gain when you sell the property** Unlike your home on which any gain is usually tax-free, the gain from selling a property which is not your only or main home is normally subject to the full blast of capital gains tax. There are some deductions you can make – the Inland Revenue★ publishes a booklet explaining the calculation of the tax due (see *Further information* below) but basically you could lose up to 40 per cent of any profit in tax.

Further information

For help comparing mortgages, see Switch with Which?★ and the FSA Comparative Tables★. You'll also find comparative details in the personal finance pages of many newspapers and on personal finance websites★. For help choosing a mortgage, consider using a mortgage broker★.

If you are interested in exploring whether to sell an endowment policy that you no longer need as an alternative to cashing it in, stopping the premiums of keeping it going, the Association of Policy Market Makers (APMM)★ can provide a list of members who can give you a quote for your policy and handle such a sale.

If you have a problem as a tenant, first try talking to your landlord. If you can't reach agreement, get advice from a local housing advice centre★, your local Citizens' Advice Bureau★ or Shelterline★. If the problem concerns unfair terms in your contract, your local Trading Standards Department★ may be able to help.

For free help and advice with debt problems, contact your local Citizens' Advice Bureau★, National Debtline★, Consumer Credit Counselling Service★ or (for England and Wales) the Community Legal Service★ which can give you contact details for a local legal centre.

To find out more about your rights if you live permanently in a mobile home, see *Mobile homes – a guide for residents and site owners* free from the Office of the Deputy Prime Minister★. For background information and to search for sites, visit the websites of Leisure and Living: Parks★ website and Quality Award Parks★. The latter is the site of residential parks which meet standards set by the National Park Homes Council (NPHC)★, a trade body committed to improving standards and whose members observe a code of practice. Contact the Camping and Caravanning Club★ for information about joining the club and a guide to its sites.

If the idea of living on a boat appeals to you, a good place to start is the Residential Boat Owners' Association (RBOA)★. Its website contains useful information and it publishes a book covering all aspects of living on a boat: *Living Afloat*. For information about licences and moorings among other matters, contact British Waterways★ or the Environment Agency★. For information about the Boat Safety Scheme, contact the Boat Safety Scheme★. For further background information, see the websites of the National Association of Boat Owners (NABO)★, Canal Junction★ and the Royal Yachting Association (RYA)★. Also browse the boating and canal magazines stocked by larger newsagents.

To find out more about communes, visit the Diggers & Dreamers★ website. If you are particularly interested in eco-friendly living, see page 142.

For background information about buy-to-let, contact the Residential Landlords Association★ which publishes a free information pack. You can also get free leaflets *Buying to let* and *Thinking of buying a residential property to let?* from the Council of Mortgage Lenders★. To check out the tax position, see free booklets IR150 *Taxation of rents – a guide to property income* and CGT1 *Capital gains tax – an introduction from the Inland Revenue*, available from the Inland Revenue★. For information about tenancy agreements, see Booklet 97 HC 228 B *Assured and assured shorthold tenancies: a guide for landlords* from the Office of the Deputy Prime Minister★.

Chapter 11

Tax and benefits

Downshifting may not cause such a big drop in income as you might expect because you may save on various job-related expenses and deductions, not least of which is income tax and National Insurance. Table 11.1 shows how these taxes change with your earnings, assuming you are an employee with fairly simple tax affairs. For example, if your earnings halve from £30,000 a year to £15,000, you'll see a fall in your tax bill of nearly £5,000 from £8,092 a year to £3,142. If downshifting means giving up highly taxed benefits, such as a company car, the reduction in your tax bill could be even bigger.

Table 11.1 How your tax bill changes with earnings in 2004–5

Before-tax earnings	Tax and National Insurance
£5,000	£54
£10,000	£1,492
£15,000	£3,142
£20,000	£4,792
£25,000	£6,442
£30,000	£8,092
£40,000	£11,258
£50,000	£15,358
£60,000	£19,458
£70,000	£23,558
£80,000	£27,658
£90,000	£31,758
£100,000	£35,858
£110,000	£39,958
£120,000	£44,058

Depending on the nature of your downshift, you may find that you can claim certain types of tax relief – for example, for the costs of running your own business and, in some circumstances, state benefits.

'*Although my gross income is considerably less, so is my expenditure and I have saved on, for example, National Insurance and superannuation.*'

Patrick

'*The real difference seems to be a positive effect that having less income meant on taxation and National Insurance contribution levels.*'

Rachel

How the income tax system works

The basics

Some types of income you get are tax-free (see overleaf), but most are taxed if your income comes to more than a certain amount, called your personal allowance. In the 2004–5 tax year, if you are under age 65 your personal allowance is £4,745. Older people have a higher allowance. A tax year runs from 6 April to the following 5 April.

Your tax bill is reduced if you can claim tax relief for money that you spend on certain items, called 'outgoings'. For example, tax relief is available for money you pay into pension arrangements, donations you make to charity through the Gift Aid scheme or payroll giving, expenses you incur running a business or renting out property, and losses you make running a business.

The tax rates

If your income is high enough for you to pay tax, you pay at one of three rates – see Table 11.2.

The main types of tax-free income

- some fringe benefits and job-related expenses, such as mileage allowance up to certain amounts, cheap or free loans up to £5,000
- up to £30,000 of compensation if you are made redundant
- lump sum (up to limits) taken as part of the benefits from a pension scheme or plan when you start to draw a pension
- working tax credit
- child benefit and child tax credit
- maternity allowance
- bereavement payment
- housing benefit and council tax benefit
- income support in some circumstances, for example, paid to a man aged 60 or over or to a single parent looking after a child
- disability living allowance
- incapacity benefit for the first 28 weeks
- income from income protection policies that pay out if you cannot work because of illness (but not such income provided by an employer)
- income from mortgage payment protection policies (that meet your mortgage interest if you cannot work because of illness or unemployment)
- interest from National Savings & Investments (NS&I) certificates
- interest from NS&I children's bonus bonds
- interest earned by investments in individual savings accounts (ISAs), pension schemes and plans, certain friendly society plans and child trust funds (CTFs). Income from share-based investments held within these arrangements is taxed at 10 per cent
- part of the income from an annuity (other than annuities bought with a pension scheme or plan)
- maintenance payments you receive
- up to £4,250 a year from taking in lodger(s) if you use the Rent-a-Room scheme
- income from fostering children up to £10,000 a year per household plus additions per child
- winnings from gambling, lotteries and premium bonds
- student grants and scholarships, and student loans.

Table 11.2 Tax rates and bands for 2004–5

Name of band	Rate of tax	Paid on this band of taxable income	Maximum tax on income in this band
Starting rate	10%	£0–£2,020	£202
Basic rate	22%[1]	£2,021–£31,400[2]	£6,463.60
Higher rate	40%[3]	Over £31,400	Unlimited

[1] But only 20% on savings income and 10% on dividends and similar income.
[2] This band is extended if you pay into certain types of pension plan or make Gift Aid donations to charity to give you relief from higher-rate tax.
[3] But 32.5% on dividends and similar income.

How tax is collected

If you work for an employer or receive an occupational or personal pension, the tax you must pay is usually collected through the Pay-As-You-Earn (PAYE) system, which means tax is deducted direct from your pay or pension before you get it.

If you have savings or investments that pay you interest, tax at a special rate, called the 'savings rate' (20 per cent in 2004–5), is often deducted from the return before you get it. If you are a basic-rate taxpayer, there is no more tax to pay. If you are a higher-rate tax-payer, you have extra tax to pay bringing the total tax up to 40 per cent. If you are a starting-rate taxpayer, you can reclaim half the tax so that you have paid at a rate of just 10 per cent. If you are a non-taxpayer, you can reclaim all the tax already deducted.

If you receive dividends from shares or similar income from share-based investments (such as unit trusts investing in shares), this income is paid with tax at a special rate of 10 per cent already deducted. If you are a basic-rate taxpayer, there is no more tax to pay. If you are a higher-rate taxpayer, you have extra tax to pay bringing the total tax up to 32.5 per cent. If you are a starting-rate taxpayer, you have paid the correct amount of tax. If you are a non-taxpayer, you cannot reclaim all the tax already deducted, so these types of investment are not very tax-efficient for you.

If you are self-employed, a partner in a firm, a higher-rate tax-payer or have untaxed income from investments, you are likely to pay at least some tax through the self-assessment system. This means you'll get a tax return shortly after the end of the tax year which you must send back by the following 31 January at the latest (see Table 11.3 on page 201).

Usually, you will have paid some tax in two instalments during the year, called 'payments on account'. The payments on account are due on 31 January during the tax year and 31 July following the tax year. Each is set equal to half your tax bill for the previous year. Once your actual tax bill for the present tax year is known, the balance of tax due (if any) must be paid by the same 31 January deadline that applies to sending in your tax return. If you have paid too much tax through the payments on account, you will receive a refund.

Under self-assessment, you are responsible for paying the correct amounts of tax at the correct times and there are fines and interest to encourage you to do this. This includes being responsible for working out your own tax bill, but provided you get your return in early enough you can ask the Inland Revenue to do the sums for you (see Table 11.3). Alternatively, if you send in your tax return through the Internet, the software automatically works out the tax due.

'There were various costs setting up the business, for example, buying a computer and photocopier. In the beginning I had an arrangement with a local estate agent to use their fax machine but, as the faxes were often 30 pages or more, it soon proved better to buy my own machine. Being a VAT-registered business, I could claim back VAT on purchases like these and also get tax relief.'

Jane

Special rules for investment-type life insurance

Some types of life insurance just pay out a lump sum or income if you die. Other types build up a cash-in value and so are used as investments. They come in all sorts of forms: regular savings plans, with-profits bonds, lump sum investment bonds, and so on.

When you invest using life insurance, you pay a lump sum or regular premiums to the life company which puts your money in an investment fund. The life company pays tax on the income and gains from the investment fund and, because of this, what is paid out to you is treated as if tax at the savings rate (20 per cent in 2004–5) has already been deducted. You can't reclaim any of this tax if you pay tax at less than the basic rate or you have unused capital

Table 11.3 Important dates in 2004–5 if you pay tax through self-assessment

Date	Why it is important	What happens if you miss the deadline
April 2004	You receive a tax return for the 2003–4 tax year that has just ended.	Not applicable.
31 July 2004	Make your second payment on account for the 2003–4 tax year.	Interest is added to the amount paid late.
30 September 2004	Get 2003–4 tax return back to your tax office if: • you want it to work out your tax bill for you, or • you owe less than £2,000 tax and want it collected through PAYE from any pay or pension you get – but see below if you file through the Internet.	• your tax office might not be able to tell you how much tax to pay in time for the 31 January deadline. • unless you file through the Internet, you'll be too late to pay the tax through PAYE.
5 October 2004	If you have not received a tax return, tell your tax office by this date if you had any income or gains in 2003–4 on which tax is due.	As well as paying the tax due, you can be charged a penalty up to the amount of tax due. You may also incur interest and other penalties if, as a result, you pay the tax late.
30 December 2004	File your tax return through the Internet if you owe less than £2,000 tax and want it collected through PAYE from any pay or pension you get.	You'll be too late to pay the tax through PAYE.
31 January 2005	• Send your 2003–4 tax return back to your tax office. • Pay any tax still due for 2003–4. • Make your first payment on account for the 2004–5 tax year.	Automatic £100 fine (or equal to the amount of tax you owe if less). • Interest is added to the unpaid tax. • Interest is added to the unpaid tax.
28 February 2005		If balance of 2003–4 tax still unpaid, a penalty equal to 5 per cent of the tax due is added to the bill.

gains tax allowance (see below). But, if you are a higher-rate tax-payer, there is often no further tax to pay. This means, in general, that life insurance investments can be tax-efficient for people who pay income tax at the higher rate and use up their capital gains tax allowance every year, but are not the best choice for other types of taxpayer.

Special rules let you take an income from many of these life insurance investments without any higher-rate tax being due at the time you take the income. The maximum income under these rules is 5 per cent of the amount you have paid in premiums (though if you don't take the full 5 per cent one year, you can carry the unused limit forward to future years). Any higher-rate tax on the income is due only when the policy matures or you cash it in. If at that time, you pay tax at less than the higher rate, there is no tax for you to pay anyway. However, the proceeds from the policy do count as part of your income for the purpose of working out tax credits (and the higher personal allowance for people aged 65 and over), so could reduce, say, the amount of child tax credit you can claim.

How the capital gains tax system works

The basics

Capital gains tax (CGT) is charged on the profit you make from selling something at a higher price than that at which you bought it (or its value when you started to own it in some other way). CGT also applies where you give something away (or dispose of it in some other way), in which case the market value of the item is used to work out the profit you are treated as having made.

However, there are various allowances and reliefs that you can claim which reduce the amount of gain on which tax is charged and may eliminate a tax bill altogether. Importantly, everyone has an annual tax-free allowance, so a large chunk of gains that would other-wise be taxable are completely tax-free. Your allowance for 2004–5 is £8,200 of gains.

Most people do not make full use of their capital gains tax allowance. If you are an income taxpayer, one way you might be able to save tax is by switching from investments that produce tax-able income to those which produce a capital gain.

Another useful CGT relief is that a gain on any 'chattel' sold (or otherwise disposed of) for less than £6,000 is tax-free. Chattels include personal possessions, paintings, antiques, jewellery, and so on. The Box lists some other tax-free gains.

Gains on things you use in a business or which count as business assets (which includes shares you acquire through an employee share scheme at work) are taxed only lightly under the CGT regime. This is a complicated area, so get advice (see 'Further information' on page 216).

Some common assets that produce tax-free gains

- your main or only home – though some of the gain may be taxable if you let out your home or use part exclusively for business
- private cars
- chattels sold for less than £6,000
- possessions with a useful life of 50 years or less (in most cases), for example, a caravan
- investment-type insurance policies – but see page 202 for how income tax might be due
- investments held in an individual savings account (ISA), personal equity plan (PEP), pension scheme or plan or child trust fund
- a lump sum taken from a pension scheme or plan when you start to draw your pension
- gilts and many corporate bonds
- winnings from betting, lotteries and premium bonds
- compensation you receive for personal injury

The tax rates

If CGT is due on any gain you make, the gain is added to your taxable income for the year and tax is charged at the rates shown in Table 11.2, except that 20 per cent tax is due on any gain (or part of a gain) falling within the basic rate band.

How tax is collected

CGT is collected through the self-assessment system – see page 199. You give details of taxable gains in your tax return. There are no payments on account and the whole CGT bill is due by 31 January following the end of the tax year in which you made the gain.

How National Insurance works

The basics

National Insurance is a tax on earnings. However, some types of National Insurance contribution entitle you to claim various state benefits (see Table 11.4). In order to protect your rights to benefits, in some situations you are credited with contributions or you have the option to pay voluntary contributions.

The rates

If you are an employee, you and your employer pay Class 1 National Insurance contributions on your earnings above the primary threshold (£4,745 in 2004–5 which is equivalent to £91 a week). The standard rate employees pay is 11 per cent of earnings up to an upper earnings limit (£31,720 or £610 a week in 2004–5) and 1 per cent of earnings above that limit.

If you earn less than £91 a week, there is nothing to pay but you are credited with contributions provided you earn at least £79 a week or its equivalent. If you earn less than that, you are not building any state benefits.

If you are self-employed, you pay Class 2 National Insurance contributions (£2.05 a week in 2004–5) which entitle you to certain state benefits. If your earnings are low (up to £4,215 a year in 2004–5), you can opt not to pay in which case you do not build up any benefits after all, but it is better not to opt out since the contributions are very low and represent good value given the benefits you build up.

Self-employed people also pay Class 4 National Insurance – this is a straightforward tax which carries no rights to benefits at all. Class 4 contributions are 8 per cent of earnings between a lower and upper profit limit (£4,745 and £31,720, respectively, in 2004–5) and 1 per cent of profits above that level.

If you have gaps in your National Insurance record – for example, for periods when you are studying or taking a sabbatical – you can opt to fill them by paying voluntary Class 3 National Insurance contributions (at £7.15 a week in 2004–5). You can go back up to six years to fill in gaps.

Some older married women and widows retain a right to pay Class 1 contributions at a lower rate (4.85 per cent of earnings between £91 and £610 a week and 1 per cent of earning above that in 2004–5) or not to pay Class 2 contributions at all. As a result, they do not build up their own entitlement to claim benefits and are expected to rely on their husband's rights.

Table 11.4 The benefits which National Insurance contributions may entitle you to claim[1]

Description of person paying	Employee	Self-employed	Voluntary payee
Type of contribution	Class 1	Class 2	Class 3
Benefits the contributions may entitle you to claim			
Contributory jobseeker's allowance	✓	✗	✗
Incapacity benefit	✓	✓	✗
State basic pension	✓	✓	✓
Bereavement benefits for spouse	✓	✓	✓

[1]You need to build up a given number of contributions over a defined period – specific rules vary from one benefit to another.

How National Insurance is collected

If you are an employee, National Insurance is taken direct from your pay before you get it through the PAYE system.

Self-employed people (sole traders and partners) must register with the Inland Revenue within three months of the end of the month in which they start self-employment to pay Class 2 contributions. Failure to register in time triggers a £100 fine. Usually, you arrange to pay Class 2 contributions by direct debit from your bank account.

The self-employed pay Class 4 contributions through the self-assessment system (see page 199). The Class 4 payments due are added to your income tax bill and collected via the payments on account and final balancing charge (or repayment) on 31 January following the end of the tax year.

National Insurance credits are usually given automatically and are triggered by your claim for certain benefits.

To arrange to pay Class 3 contributions, contact your local tax office. The precise arrangements will depend on whether you are paying for the current year or filling in gaps in previous years.

The main state benefits you might be able to claim

The UK has a complex but reasonably comprehensive state safety net that may provide you with some financial help in certain circumstances.

Table 11.5 lists the main benefits available and when they might apply. They can broadly be divided into three groups:

- **means-tested** Benefits which you can claim only if your income and savings are low
- **contributory** Benefits for which you build up entitlement by paying National Insurance
- **non-contributory** Benefits that anyone can claim, regardless of their income, savings or contributions record.

See below for a brief outline of each benefit. Check the Box on page 207 to see which benefits are tax-free. The rules for state benefits are extremely complicated and rates change frequently, often at short notice. While the amounts given here are correct at the time of going to press, you are advised to check what you are entitled to with the relevant authority. If you think you might be eligible, contact the body responsible for administering claims (see Table 11.5) or see 'Further information' on page 216 for advice on how to get more details.

Access to learning grants

If you are a student, you may be eligible for a grant or loan to help with specific costs or more generally to ease financial difficulties. Your college administers these funds and decides how much to give you.

Bereavement benefits

Benefits are payable to your widow or widower and, in the case of widowed parent's allowance to an unmarried partner of the opposite

Table 11.5 Summary of main state benefits

Name of benefit	Who it is for	Type of benefit	Who to contact if you want to claim
Access to learning grants	Students	Means-tested	Your college
Bereavement benefits	Husband or wife of someone who has died	Contributory (deceased's record)	Job Centre Plus
Carer's allowance	People caring for someone who is disabled or elderly	Non-contributory	Job Centre Plus/ The Pension Service
Child benefit	Families with children	Non-contributory	Inland Revenue
Council tax benefit	Council taxpayers on a low income	Means-tested	Local authority
Child tax credit	Families with children	Means-tested	Inland Revenue
Disability living allowance	People of working age with a disability	Non-contributory	Job Centre Plus
Housing benefit	People paying rent and on a low income	Means-tested	Local authority
Other housing costs (via income support or jobseeker's allowance)	People paying a mortgage and on a low income	Means-tested	Job Centre Plus/ The Pension Service
Incapacity benefit	People unable to work because of illness or disability	Contributory and means-tested	Job Centre Plus
Income support	People on a low income and unavailable for work	Means-tested	Job Centre Plus/ The Pension Service
Jobseeker's allowance	Unemployed	Contributory or means-tested	Job Centre Plus
Maternity allowance	Expectant and new mothers	[1]	Job Centre Plus
Retirement pension	People over state pension age	Contributory	The Pension Service
Statutory maternity, paternity or adoption pay	Employees expecting or with a new child	[1]	Your employer
Statutory sick pay	Employees off work sick	[1]	Your employer
Student fees (help with), student loans and grants	Students	Means-tested	Local Education Authority
Working tax credit	People in work on a low income or with childcare costs or with a disability	Means-tested	Inland Revenue

[1] Entitlement depends on earning at least a given amount and having worked for a certain length of time.

sex provided you had built up a sufficient National Insurance record. The recipient must be under state pension age. There are three benefits:

- **bereavement payment** A tax-free lump sum of £2,000
- **widowed parent's allowance** A flat-rate income (£79.60 a week in 2004–5) for a widow, widower or unmarried partner caring for one or more children
- **bereavement allowance** A temporary income (from £23.88 a week to £79.60 a week in 2004–5 depending on the age of the widow or widower) payable where the widow or widower is aged 45 or over and is not caring for children. It is payable for a maximum of 52 weeks.

Bereavement benefits stop if the recipient remarries or starts to live with someone as husband and wife.

Carer's allowance

This provides an income for people who spend 35 hours a week or more caring for someone who is disabled (and in receipt of either disability living allowance or attendance allowance – see below). It is paid at a single rate (£44.35 a week in 2004–5).

Child benefit

This is a flat-rate amount (£16.50 a week for the eldest child and £11.05 for each subsequent child in 2004–5) you get if you are caring for one or more children.

If you have been a single parent since before 6 June 1998 and were already receiving child benefit on that date, you get a higher amount for your first child (£17.55 a week). This higher rate is lost if you marry or start to live with someone as husband and wife.

Child tax credit and working tax credit

If you have children, you may be eligible for both child tax credit (CTC) and working tax credit (WTC) or just CTC. In either case, the benefits are not just restricted to low-income households. You can qualify for at least some CTC even if your household income is as high as £58,175 in 2004–5 (or £66,350 if you have a child under age one).

If you have no children, you may be able to claim WTC if you work but your income is low, you can't work because of disability or you are aged 50 or more and have recently started work after a period claiming certain state benefits.

WTC and CTC are integrated and you make a single claim for both benefits. The amount you get depends on how many elements – see Table 11.6 – you qualify for, and your income is worked out in broadly the same way as for tax purposes. You add together the relevant elements then, for every £1 by which your income exceeds a first threshold (£5,060 in 2004–5), your WTC and the individual element(s) of CTC are reduced by 37p. WTC is reduced first with the childcare element last, then the CTC. If you qualify only for CTC, the threshold at which you start to lose the individual elements of CTC is higher (£13,480 in 2004–5).

Any household with children may qualify for the family element of CTC. But this is reduced when the household's income reaches a second threshold (£50,000 in 2004–5). You lose £1 of credit for every £15 of income over the threshold.

Table 11.6   Tax credits in 2004–5

Element	Amount
Working tax credit	
Basic (applies to all claimants)	£1,570
Lone parent or couple	£1,545
Working 30-hour per week	£640
Disabled worker	£2,100
Severe disability	£890
50-plus working 16–29 hours per week	£1,075
50-plus working 30+ hours per week	£1,610
Childcare: 70% of eligible costs which are up to £135 a week	Maximum
for one child and £200 a week for two or more	£7,280
Child tax credit	
Individual element per child (increased if child disabled or severely disabled)	£1,445
Family element	£545
Family element if you have a child under age one	£1,090

Council tax benefit

This covers part or all of your council tax bill if your income and savings are low. The benefit is paid as a reduction in your bill. You get this benefit automatically if you are getting income support or non-contributory jobseeker's allowance (see below) but can also be eligible if you are not getting these benefits.

Separately, you may qualify for a discount on your bill if you are the only adult in your household (25 per cent reduction) or you have a disability for which the house has special features (property taxed at one band below its actual band). These discounts are not means-tested. In assessing the number of adults in the household, some are ignored, for example, full-time higher education students and carers providing care for at least 35 hours a week.

Disability living allowance

This is a flat-rate weekly income for people under state pension age who require help with personal care or continual supervision for their safety and/or have mobility problems. The care component is paid at one of three rates (£15.55 a week, £39.35 or £58.80 in 2004–5) depending on the extent of help or supervision required. The mobility component is paid at one of two rates (£15.55 a week or £41.05 in 2004–5).

The allowance can be paid indefinitely up to state pension age. (Older people who require help with care can claim attendance allowance instead.)

Housing benefit

This covers part or all of your rent if your income and savings are low. The benefit is either paid as a rebate if you are a council tenant or as cash if you rent privately. You get this benefit automatically if you are getting income support or non-contributory jobseeker's allowance (see below) but can also be eligible if you are not getting these benefits.

The amount you get may be reduced if your rent is deemed to be overlyexpensive.

Other housing costs

If your income and savings are low, you might qualify for help with your mortgage payments through either income support or non-contributory jobseeker's allowance. The benefit will cover only the interest payments, not any capital repayments, so you may need to ask your lender to waive any capital repayments for the time being.

If you took out your mortgage before 2 October 1995, your interest payments will not be met at all for the first eight weeks of your claim. For the next 18 weeks, income support or jobseeker's allowance will meet half the cost but based on a standard interest rate that might be less than you are actually paying and covering only the first £100,000 of your loan. After that, the whole of the interest payments is covered but still only based on the standard interest rate and a maximum £100,000 borrowed.

Where you took out your mortgage on or after 2 October 1995, you get no help with your mortgage for the first 39 weeks of your claim. After that, the whole of the interest payments is covered but based on the standard interest rate and maximum £100,000 loan as described above.

The help you get may also be reduced if your housing costs are considered excessive – for example, because your home is deemed to be much larger than you need.

Incapacity benefit

If you are unable to work because of illness and you do not qualify for statutory sick pay (see below), you may instead be able to claim incapacity benefit. This has three elements:

- **short-term incapacity benefit at the lower rate** (£55.90 a week in 2004–5) payable for the first 28 weeks. (But no benefit is payable for the first three days of illness)
- **short-term incapacity benefit at the higher rate** (£66.15 a week in 2004–5) payable for the next 24 weeks
- **long-term incapacity benefit** (£74.15 a week in 2004–5) payable after 52 weeks. You qualify for an age addition if you are under age 45 when you start to claim.

You may be able to claim extra for dependants. If you also receive an income from a pension arrangement or income protection insurance (in other words, insurance designed to replace part of your earnings in the event of illness), your incapacity benefit is reduced by 50p for each £1 by which this other income amounts to more than £85 a week.

Income support

This may be claimed if your income and savings are low and you are not required to be available for work, for example because you are a single parent looking after a child, a carer or a disabled student. (Otherwise, people of working age would normally claim job-seeker's allowance instead – see below.)

You will not be eligible if you have capital (savings, investments and so on but not including the value of your home) of more than £8,000 (£12,000 if you are aged 60 or more). Capital of more than £3,000 (£6,000 if aged 60 or more) will reduce the amount of bene-fit you can get.

The rules are complicated but basically the amount you need to live on (your 'applicable amount') is worked out by adding together various elements depending on your circumstances, for example, whether you are single or a couple, have children, have a disability, and so on. The amount for a single person aged 25 or over with no other additions in 2004–5 is £55.65 a week.

Your income (with an addition to allow for income you are deemed to get from savings over a given limit) is worked out and subtracted from your applicable amount. The amount by which your income falls short of the applicable amount is the amount of benefit you get.

If you are a tenant, income support does not cover your rent but you are likely also to qualify for housing benefit. If you have a mort-gage, income support might pay some or all of your mortgage inter-est – see 'Other housing costs' above.

Jobseeker's allowance

This is payable if you become unemployed. It has two elements:

- **contributory** A flat-rate benefit (£55.65 a week in 2004–5 if you are 25 or over) paid for a maximum of six months. Only Class 1 contributions help you qualify and the required num-ber must have been paid/credited over the two years before you claim
- **income-based** Worked out in a similar way to income support (see above) and payable indefinitely.

To qualify, you must be under state pension age and available for work.

Maternity allowance

You may be able to claim this if you do not qualify for statutory maternity pay (see below) and you have been an employee or self-employed for at least 26 of the 66 weeks before the baby is due. You must be earning at least a minimum amount (£30 a week in 2004–5) during the 13 weeks immediately prior to starting your maternity leave.

The allowance is payable for a maximum 26 weeks and paid at a standard rate (£102.80 a week in 2004–5).

Retirement pension

This is payable once you reach state pension age (65 for men and 60 to 65 for women). The standard flat-rate basic pension is £79.60 a week for a single person in 2004–5, but you might be entitled to additional amounts. See Chapter 12 for more information.

Statutory maternity, paternity or adoption pay

Statutory maternity pay (SMP) is paid to you by your employer. Eligibility does not depend on paying National Insurance but you must be earning at least the 'lower earnings limit' (£79 a week in 2004–5) and you must have worked continuously for your employer during the 26 weeks up to the 15th week before the baby is due. SMP is paid for a maximum of 26 weeks. This is made up of six weeks at a higher rate equal to 90 per cent of your normal pay and 20 weeks at a standard rate (£102.80 a week in 2004–5).

If you earn less than the lower earnings limit, you may instead be able to claim maternity allowance (see above).

Statutory adoption pay (SAP) is similar to SMP and payable to a mother who newly adopts a child. SAP is also available to fathers but then similar to statutory paternity pay (SPP). SPP is payable for a maximum of two weeks at the lower of 90 per cent of normal pay or a standard rate (£102.80 a week in 2004–5). The qualifying conditions (length of time with employer and earning at least the lower earnings limit) are basically the same as those for SMP.

Statutory sick pay

Statutory sick pay (SSP) is paid to you by your employer. Eligibility does not depend on paying National Insurance but you must be earning at least the 'lower earnings limit' (£79 a week in 2004–5).

SSP is payable at a standard rate (£66.15 a week in 2004–5) for a maximum of 28 weeks. (It is not payable for the first three days of illness.) If you are still unable to work after that, you may instead be able to claim incapacity benefit (see above).

Your employer may operate his or her own sick pay scheme with more generous payments.

Student fees (help with), student loans and grants

Under the system in place at the time of writing, students must normally pay fees (£1,150 a year in 2004–5) towards their tuition costs but this contribution is means-tested, so you might pay less or nothing at all. How much you must pay depends on your income (or your household income if you live with a spouse or partner) but ignoring various amounts, including any earnings from casual or part-time jobs you do while studying and during the holidays.

From autumn 2006 onwards, top-up fees are due to be introduced (if the legislation, which is at the time of writing being debated by Parliament, reaches the statute book). You may then have to pay up to £3,000 a year in tuition fees but can fund this by taking out extra student loans through a new Graduate Contribution Scheme. However, if your household income is low, the government may pay the first slice of the fees (£1,150 at 2004–5 rates) and universities will be encouraged to make more bursaries available to poorer students.

Tuition fees – Scotland

There are no tuition fees if both your home and place of study are in Scotland. Instead you may have to pay a Graduate Endowment after graduation. This is a one-off lump-sum payment, currently around £2,000. You can take out a student loan to cover this payment.

To help you with your living costs while a student, you can take out student loans. Table 11.7 shows the maximum loans available in 2004–5. A quarter of the maximum loan is available only to students on a low income. The remaining three-quarters of the maximum student loan is available regardless of your income.

From 2004–5, the government intends to reintroduce student grants (to be called the 'higher education grant') for people from low-income households. Students whose household income is less than £15,200 a year can apply for a £1,000 grant in 2004–5. Where household income is up to £21,185, you can get a reduced grant and above that threshold no grant at all.

You do not start to repay student loans until after the end of your course, and the loans are 'income contingent'. This means you make repayments only if your income exceeds a set threshold, currently £10,000 a year but due to rise to £15,000 from April 2005. You repay at a rate of 9 per cent of your income above the threshold. Repayments are collected through the tax system (by PAYE if you are an employee or self-assessment if you are self-employed – see page 000). There is no interest as such on the money you owe in student loans. Instead the amount outstanding is increased each year in line with inflation. This means student loans will generally be a good deal cheaper than any other form of borrowing.

To encourage a supply of graduates to fill key public sector jobs, the government funds various financial packages for people training to be teachers, health professionals, and so on.

For more details about the help available to mature students, see Chapter 4, page 66.

Table 11.7 Maximum student loans available in 2004–5[1]

	Overall maximum available	Maximum non-means-tested amount	Maximum means-tested amount
Full-year rates (i.e. each year apart from the final year)			
Studying in London	£5,050	£3,970	£1,260
Studying elsewhere	£4,095	£3,070	£1,025
Final-year rates			
Studying in London	£4,380	£3,285	£1,095
Studying elsewhere	£3,555	£2,665	£890

[1] Lower amounts are available to students who live with their parents.

> '*If we were going back to school we would need to fund it and make use of any available support ... We would be eligible for a student loan and the local authority should pick up the tuition fees under current rules.*'
>
> John and Jenny

Further information

Tax, National Insurance, tax credits and child benefit are all administered by the Inland Revenue★. You can get information about any of these areas by contacting your local tax office, the tax office that normally deals with you, the various Inland Revenue helplines or the Inland Revenue website. A large range of leaflets and booklets are available, some of which are listed in Table 11.8.

Many state benefits are administered by the Department for Work and Pensions (DWP)★ which also publishes a range of free leaflets and booklets – see Table 11.8 for a selection of these. At the local level, the DWP's work is done by either JobCentre Plus★ offices if you are of working age or The Pension Service★ if you have reached state pension age or you are looking ahead to benefits in retirement.

A few benefits, in particular housing benefit and council tax benefit, are handled by your local authority★ and, if you are a student, you need to contact your Local Education Authority★ or you can download information from the websites of the Department for Education and Skills (DfES)★ and the Student Loans Company★.

Table 11.8 Selected free information leaflets and booklets

Reference number	Title	Who publishes it?
IR60	Students and the Inland Revenue	Inland Revenue
IR87	Letting and your home (including the Rent a Room scheme etc)	Inland Revenue
IR110	Bank and building society interest. A guide for savers	Inland Revenue
IR115	Income tax, National Insurance and childcare	Inland Revenue
IR150	Taxation of rents – a guide to property income	Inland Revenue
IR2008	ISAs, PEPs and TESSAs	Inland Revenue
P/SE/1	Thinking of working for yourself?	Inland Revenue
SA/BK8	Self-assessment. Your guide	Inland Revenue
P3	Understanding your tax code	Inland Revenue
CA01	National Insurance for employees	Inland Revenue
CA02	National Insurance for self-employed people with small earnings	Inland Revenue
CA 08	Voluntary National Insurance contributions	Inland Revenue
CA13	National Insurance contributions for married women with reduced elections	Inland Revenue
CGT1	Capital gains tax – an introduction	Inland Revenue
E15	Pay and time off work for parents	Inland Revenue
BC2	Expecting a baby?	DWP
BC3	Bringing up children?	DWP
N117A	Guide to maternity benefits	DWP
WTC1	Child tax credit and working tax credit. An introduction	Inland Revenue
WTC5	Child tax credit and working tax credit. Help with the cost of childcare	Inland Revenue
DS704	Disability living allowance	DWP
GL14	Widowed?	DWP
GL16	Help with your rent	DWP
GL17	Help with your council tax	DWP
GL23	Social security benefit rates	DWP
HB5	A guide to non-contributory benefits for disabled people and their carers	DWP
IB1	A guide to incapacity benefit	DWP
SD2	Sick or unable to work?	DWP
SD3	Long term ill or disabled	DWP
SD4	Caring for someone?	DWP
S/FSHE/V4	Financial support for higher education students 2004/05	
S/BTGB/V4	Bridging the gap: a guide to the disabled students' allowances in higher education in 2004/05	DfES[1]
S/CCGB/V4	Childcare grant and other support for student parents in higher education in 2004/05	DfES[1]
S/SLTC/V4	Student loans: a guide to terms and conditions	DfES[1]

[1]Can be downloaded from DfES website but for hard copy contact your Local education Authority.

Chapter 12

Pensions

It's not just the income you have to live on today that might be affected by downshifting. It can also have a big impact on the income that you will have to live on in retirement, even if this is many years away. You need to be aware of this and the steps you might take to protect your eventual retirement income. And, if your downshift involves taking early retirement, you need to know when you can claim your various pensions and how much pension you will get.

Chapters 3 to 8 explain how each type of downshift might affect your pension or pension rights. This chapter fills in the detail about how different pension arrangements work. It considers in turn the three main types of pension you might get: state pensions, occupational pensions and personal pensions (including stakeholder schemes).

'My biggest concern was whether I could still afford to maintain my monthly savings as planning for an adequate income in retirement is important to me. On the face of it, it seemed doubtful I could do so at the same level. I projected forward already earned, and prospective, employer and state pensions and reviewed my investments and concluded that a savings drop would not be too critical ... the surprise was that the [switch to a] part-time salary really made no difference to my standard of living ... I was able to keep saving at more or less the same level as before, and two years on was able to do more.'

Rachel

State pensions

There are two main state pensions: the basic pension which virtually everyone is entitled to and the state additional pension, restricted to employees and a few other groups.

State pensions become payable from state pension age, which is 65 for all men and for women born on or after 6 March 1955. For women born before 6 April 1950, it is age 60. For women born between those two dates, it lies between 60 and 65 – see Box below. You can start your pension later in which case the amount you get is increased – see page 226.

You do not have to stop work to be eligible to start receiving your state pension.

Women's changing state pension age

If you were born between 6 April 1950 and 5 March 1955 inclusive you are caught by transitional rules as women's state pension age is raised from the current 60 to age 65. To work out your own retirement age, count the number of full and part pension months that your birth date falls after 6 April 1950. (A pension month runs from the sixth day of one month to the fifth day of the next.) Add the result to age 60 to find your pension age. For example, if you were born on 7 May 1953, your birthdate is 38 pension months after 6 April 1950 (including the part-month from 6 to 7 May). Therefore, your state pension age is 60 + 38 months = 63 years 2 months.

State basic pension

The amount you get on reaching state pension age depends on the record of National Insurance that you have built up during your working life. 'Working life' means the tax years from the one in which you reach 16 to the last full tax year before you reach state pension age. A tax year runs from 6 April to the following 5 April.

You build up your record by paying some types of National Insurance contributions if you are earning or by being credited with contributions in certain circumstances. Table 12.1 summarises the main circumstances in which you will be building up your record.

Each year that counts is called a 'qualifying year'. For details of the amount you must pay, see Chapter 11.

The length of your working life and the number of years which are qualifying determines the proportion of the full basic pension that you will get – see Table 12.2.

Provided you have paid or been credited with National Insurance contributions for at least a quarter of your working life,

---

Home responsibilities protection

If you stay at home to look after a child or to care for someone who is disabled, you may be eligible for home responsibilities protection (HRP). This is not quite the same as contribution credits. In the case of the state basic pension, complete years (but not part years) for which you get HRP are removed from your working life, so you need fewer qualifying years for any given level of basic pension. In the case of the state second pension, you build up the pension as if you had earnings equal to the low earnings threshold (£11,600 in 2004–5).

HRP for the state basic pension is given automatically if you are not earning but receiving child benefit. It is also given automatically for the state second pension if you're not earning and getting child benefit but only while your child is under age six. If you are a couple, you might want to think about which of you should claim the child benefit.

In general, HRP for the state second pension is not available if your child is older than six, but may be if he or she has a disability. In that case you will need to put in a claim for HRP.

You may be able to claim HRP if you spend at least 35 hours a week caring for someone who gets state benefits because of their disability (for example, attendance allowance) and you are not yourself getting (or eligible for) carer's allowance or certain other state benefits.

To make an HRP claim, get form CF411 from the Inland Revenue*. For tax years from 2002–3 onwards, you must claim within three years of the end of the year to which the HRP applies. There is no time limit for earlier years.

---

you'll normally get at least some state basic pension. And, provided roughly nine-tenths of your working life is made up of qualifying years, you'll get the maximum pension.

In 2004–5, the maximum state basic pension for a single person is £79.60 a week. If a couple have each built up a state pension in their own right, they could get up to double this amount between them. If it would be more than a wife (or a husband from 2010 onwards) can get based on her (his) own National Insurance record, she (he) can claim a pension up to £47.65 a week based on her (his) spouse's National Insurance record.

Table 12.1   Main circumstances in which you will be building up state basic pension in 2004–5

National Insurance status	Who this applies to	Comments
Credited with contributions while employee on low earnings	Employee earning between £79 and £91 a week	Employees earning less than £79 a week are not building up state pension
Paying Class 1 contributions	Employee earning more than £91 a week	Married women paying at the reduced rate are not building up state pension
Paying Class 2 contributions	Self-employed or partner	People with earnings below £4,215, and some married women, can choose not to pay but then are not building up state pension
Paying Class 3 contributions	Anyone not required to pay contributions and not receiving credits who chooses to pay	You can go back up to six years to fill gaps in your record
Credited with contributions while unemployed[1]	You are claiming certain benefits, such as jobseeker's allowance	If you are a man aged 60 to 64, contributions are automatically credited without need to claim benefits
Credited with contributions while unable to work because of illness or disability[1]	You are claiming certain benefits, such as incapacity benefit, or entitled to statutory sick pay	
Credited with contributions while on maternity leave[1]	You are claiming maternity allowance or entitled to statutory maternity pay	
Credited with contributions while still in further education[1]	Automatic credits if you are aged 16 to 18 and still learning	But no credits while you are in higher education (for example, at university)

[1]Whether or not you qualify for credits usually depends on meeting various conditions, so check with your JobCentre Plus office that you are protected.

Table 12.2 How much state basic pension a single person might get[1]

Number of qualifying years you've built up	If your working life is 44 years (most women born before 6 April 1950)		If your working life is 49 years (all men and most women born after 5 March 1955)	
	Percentage of full basic pension you get	Weekly pension at 2004–5 rate	Percentage of full basic pension you get	Weekly pension at 2004–5 rate
9 or less	0	£0.00	0	£0.00
10	26	£20.70	0	£0.00
11	29	£23.08	25	£19.90
12	31	£24.68	28	£22.29
13	34	£27.06	30	£23.88
14	36	£28.66	32	£25.47
15	39	£31.04	35	£27.86
16	42	£33.43	37	£29.45
17	44	£35.02	39	£31.04
18	47	£37.41	41	£32.64
19	49	£39.00	44	£35.02
20	52	£41.39	46	£36.62
21	54	£42.98	48	£38.21
22	57	£45.37	50	£39.80
23	59	£46.96	53	£42.19
24	62	£49.35	55	£43.78
25	65	£51.74	57	£45.37
26	67	£53.33	60	£47.76
27	70	£55.72	62	£49.35
28	72	£57.31	64	£50.94
29	75	£59.70	66	£52.54
30	77	£61.29	69	£54.92
31	80	£63.68	71	£56.52
32	83	£66.07	73	£58.11
33	85	£67.66	75	£59.70
34	88	£70.05	78	£62.09
35	90	£71.64	80	£63.68
36	93	£74.03	82	£65.27
37	95	£75.62	85	£67.66
38	98	£78.01	87	£69.25
39	100	£79.60	89	£70.84
40	100	£79.60	91	£72.44
41	100	£79.60	94	£74.82
42	100	£79.60	96	£76.42
43	100	£79.60	98	£78.01
44 or more	100	£79.60	100	£79.60

[1] Assuming a working life of 44 or 49 years. If you qualify for home responsibilities protection, your working life may be shorter and this table does not then apply.

State additional pension

On top of any state basic pension, you might also be building up state additional pension. The amount of pension you get depends on your earnings averaged over your working life.

Before 6 April 2002, the additional pension was called the state earnings-related pension (SERPS); since then, it has been recast as the state second pension (S2P). This was more than just a name change. There were also changes to the groups of people who could build up additional pension and to the way it was calculated with more generous pension rights for people on low incomes. However, you are not building up state additional pension if your earnings are very low (less £79 a week in 2004–5) and self-employed people are excluded from the scheme altogether.

Table 12.3 shows who may be building up state additional pension. But, if you are an employee you may be 'contracted out', in which case you will not currently be adding to your state additional pension. Instead you will be building up an equivalent pension through an occupational pension scheme at work or through your own personal pension.

Working out how much state additional pension you might get is very complicated. You can find details in *Planning your pension* published by Which? Books★. But we recommend that you do not try to work out your own entitlement. Instead ask for a state retirement pension forecast or check the amount on your combined benefit statement – see 'Further information' on page 239. In September 2003, the average additional pension being paid out to current pensioners was £11.16 a week.

Impact of downshifting on your state pension

The impact of a downshift on your state pension depends largely on the nature of your move. But there may be steps you can take to mitigate the effects. Chart 12.1 summarises the most common situations.

Stopping work altogether

If you stop work, you will either create a gap in your National Insurance record or your record may be protected, depending on the reason for not working. For example, if you take a break from work in order to care for a child, you are likely to qualify for HRP

Table 12.3 Main circumstances in which you are building up state additional pension in 2004–5

National Insurance status	Who this applies to	Comments
Paying or treated as paying Class 1 contributions	Employee earning more than £79 a week	• Employees earning less than £79 a week and married women paying at the reduced rate are not building up state additional pension • Employees earning between £79 a week (£4,108 a year) and £11,800 a year build up additional pension as if they were earning £11,600 a year
Credited with entitlement while caring for young child	Carers who are not working and are entitled to child benefit for a child under age six	These groups all build up additional pension as if they have earnings of £11,600 a year
Credited with entitlement while caring for someone else	Carers entitled to carer's allowance because they are looking after someone who is elderly or disabled	
Credited with entitlement while unable to work because of your own illness or disability	People entitled to long-term incapacity benefit, provided they are in the workforce for at least a tenth of their working life.	

(see page 220). Some carers also qualify for HRP. If you have to stop work because of illness or unemployment, you may qualify for National Insurance credits (see page 221). Often you'll get HRP or credits automatically but check this (see 'Further information' on page 239), if you're not certain that's happening in your case. Apart from this, there is nothing more you need to do to protect your state pension in these circumstances.

Credits protect only your entitlement to state basic pension, not additional pension. But if you fall within one of the groups listed in Table 12.3, you may, despite not working, be building up additional pension too.

If you stop work for some other reason – for example, to travel – you will not qualify for credits and the break will create a gap in your National Insurance record. You can pay voluntary Class 3 National Insurance contributions to fill such a gap, but first you need to check whether this is worthwhile. As Table 12.2 shows, you can have gaps totalling up to about a tenth of the years in your working life (usually five years) without causing any reduction in your state basic pension. So, if your career break would not take your total breaks above that limit, there is no advantage in paying Class 3 contributions. But you normally have only six years within which to decide whether to pay these contributions. If you still have a lot of your working life ahead of you, you'll need to estimate whether you might develop further gaps in your National Insurance record in the years ahead – if you're not sure, you might want to pay the voluntary contributions just in case. And bear in mind that, if you went to university, the typical course will have already resulted in a gap of three years in your record unless you chose to plug it with voluntary contributions (which most people don't).

Table 12.4 shows the amount you must pay in 2004–5 if you go back to plug gaps in your record. With recent gaps, you are treated as simply paying late and the rate is that which applied in the year concerned. When filling more distant gaps, you usually pay at the current rate. Unlike HRP, Class 3 contributions can be used to fill gaps that are just part-years as well as full years.

Normally you can go back only six years to fill gaps. However, since 1998, the Inland Revenue has failed to send out warning letters as it should have done to people with gaps in their record. To correct this error, the time limit for filling the gaps concerned has been extended to 5 April 2008 (or in some cases 5 April 2009) and even the more distant gaps can be filled at the original rate.

Reducing the hours you work

If your downshift involves cutting your hours of work, you will still be building up state basic pension unless your earnings fall below the lower earnings limit (£4,745 a year – equivalent to £79 a week in 2004–5). You might be reducing the amount of state additional pension you'll eventually get. But if your earnings both before and after the downshift are at least £4,108 a year and no more than £11,600 at 2004–5 rates (and assuming you are not contracted out), you will be building up additional pension at the same rate.

Table 12.4 What you pay in Class 3 National Insurance
contributions in 2004–5

Year to which contribution applies	Contributions paid in 2004–5	
	Weekly rate under the normal rules	Weekly rate if you are affected by the Inland Revenue error
2004–5	£7.15	£7.15
2003–4	£6.95	£6.95
2002–3	£6.85	£6.85
2001–2	£7.15	£6.75
2000–1	£7.15	£6.55
1999–2000	£7.15	£6.45
1998–9	£7.15	£6.25
1997–8	Not applicable	£6.05

Running your own business

If you switch from employment to being your own boss (either self-employed on your own account or in partnership with others), you will still be building up state basic pension provided you are paying Class 2 National Insurance contributions. These contributions are very good value (at just £2.05 a week in 2004–5), so think carefully before opting out of paying them if your profits are low.

Self-employed people are not eligible at all for state additional pension.

Rather than being self-employed, you might decide to run your own business as a company. A director of a company counts as an employee for tax and National Insurance purposes. You have the flexibility to pay yourself either salary, dividends or both. Bear in mind that, provided you pay yourself at least £79 a week (£4,108 a year) at 2004–5 rates, you will be building up state additional pension as if you are earning £11,600 a year as well as state basic pension.

Deferring your state pension

There is no real scope to use your state pension to help fund your downshift because you can never start to draw this pension before state pension age (see page 219).

However, you can delay the start of your state pension in which case the amount you receive will be increased. This might be a useful boost to your eventual retirement income if you will face a reduced state pension because of gaps in your National Insurance

Chart 12.1   How downshifting may affect your state pension

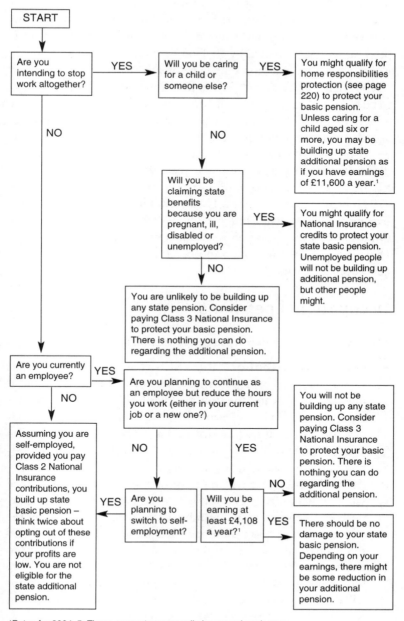

START

Are you intending to stop work altogether? — **YES** → Will you be caring for a child or someone else? — **YES** → You might qualify for home responsibilities protection (see page 220) to protect your basic pension. Unless caring for a child aged six or more, you may be building up state additional pension as if you have earnings of £11,600 a year.[1]

NO

Will you be claiming state benefits because you are pregnant, ill, disabled or unemployed? — **YES** → You might qualify for National Insurance credits to protect your state basic pension. Unemployed people will not be building up additional pension, but other people might.

NO

You are unlikely to be building up any state pension. Consider paying Class 3 National Insurance to protect your basic pension. There is nothing you can do regarding the additional pension.

Are you currently an employee? — **YES** → Are you planning to continue as an employee but reduce the hours you work (either in your current job or a new one?)

NO

Assuming you are self-employed, provided you pay Class 2 National Insurance contributions, you build up state basic pension – think twice about opting out of these contributions if your profits are low. You are not eligible for the state additional pension.

NO → Are you planning to switch to self-employment? — **YES** →

YES → Will you be earning at least £4,108 a year?[1] — **NO** → You will not be building up any state pension. Consider paying Class 3 National Insurance to protect your basic pension. There is nothing you can do regarding the additional pension.

— **YES** → There should be no damage to your state basic pension. Depending on your earnings, there might be some reduction in your additional pension.

[1]Rates for 2004–5. These amounts are usually increased each year.

227

record or you will have only a low pension from other sources because of your downshift (see below).

At the time of writing, the rules are in the process of being changed. Under the new system, from 6 April 2005, your state pension will be increased by 10.4 per cent for each year that you do not claim it after reaching state pension age. You can defer the start of your pension for as long as you like. You will also be able to elect to take the increase as a taxable lump sum instead of extra pension.

Whether deferring your state pension would be a good option for you depends on how long you live after retirement. For example, based on the 2004–5 full state basic pension rate, a person who defers his or her pension for five years would give up $5 \times 52 \times £79.60 = £20,696$. This would earn an increase of $5 \times 10.4\% \times £79.60 = £41.32$ a week or £2,152 a year. The person would have to live another $£20,696/£2,152 = 9.6$ years to break even on the deal. On average, a man aged 65 would be expected to live for another 15.6 years and a woman of 65 another 18.8 years, so deferral looks a good deal at that age.

Occupational pensions

There are essentially two types of occupational pension scheme:

- **defined contribution**, also called 'money purchase'. This works like a personal savings scheme. Money goes in, is invested for you and the fund that has built up by retirement is used to provide your pension – often by buying a special product called an annuity (see Box on page 229). Thus the pension you get depends on the amount paid into the scheme, investment growth, charges, and annuity rates at retirement.

- **defined benefit**, of which the most common type is the 'final salary' scheme. Your pension is worked out according to a formula and depends on the number of years you have been in the scheme, your pay over some specified period and a fraction called the 'accrual rate'. For example, you might get a pension equal to one-eighteenth of your average pay over the last three years before retirement for each year of membership. If your average pay was £30,000 and you had been in the scheme 20 years, your pension would be $20 \times 1/80 \times £30,000 = £7,500$ a year.

In a hybrid scheme, your pension is worked out on both a defined contribution and a defined benefit basis and you receive whichever amount is the greater.

Whatever the type of scheme, it may be contributory (you pay something towards the cost of your pension, typically around 5 per cent of your salary) or non-contributory (your employer pays the full cost). Either way, by law your employer is required to pay a substantial part of the cost.

Final salary schemes have had a bad press in recent times because some schemes have been wound up but were short of funds, leaving members with much smaller pensions than they had expected (or in the worst cases, no pension at all). However, this

---

Annuities

An annuity is an investment where you exchange a lump sum for an income. In the case of annuities used for pensions, the income is payable for the rest of your life. Once you have bought the annuity you cannot generally get your lump sum back, though there are variants which guarantee at least some minimum return should you die within a few years of purchase.

The income from a traditional annuity is set for life at the time you buy. So, once you have bought an annuity, any subsequent changes in annuity rates do not affect you at all. In many cases, the income will be a level amount each year, but other annuities have built-in yearly increases. The younger you are when you buy an annuity, the lower the income you get (because the longer it is expected that the income will have to be paid out). For example, at the time of writing, £10,000 could buy a level income of £739 a year for a man aged 65 but only £578 a year for a man aged 55. Instead of a traditional annuity, you could opt for an investment-linked annuity where the income you get goes up and down depending on the performance of an underlying fund of investments. However, these are more risky than traditional annuities and only suitable if you have a fairly large pension fund to invest or you have other sources of income to fall back on.

has affected a minority of schemes and, in general, defined benefit schemes can be the best type of scheme for many people. This is because your employer, rather than you, bears what is called the 'investment risk' – in other words, the risk that the invested contributions will enjoy only poor growth or fall in value, meaning that extra has to be paid into the scheme to fund the level of pension promised by the formula. By contrast, in a money purchase scheme, you bear the investment risk: so if your pension fund has grown poorly by the time you want to start drawing an income, you get a smaller pension.

Investment risk means that an employer running a final salary scheme faces a potentially large and variable bill. So final salary schemes are generally offered only by larger employers and are common in the public sector (where, at the end of the day, taxpayers can be called on to foot any extra bill). If you work for a smaller employer, any occupational scheme is most likely to be a money purchase one.

Impact of downshifting on your occupational pension

Again, the impact depends importantly on the nature of your downshift.

Stopping work altogether without starting your pension

If you stop work altogether, you will cease to be an active member of your employer's pension scheme. This means no new contributions will be paid into the scheme by either you or your employer on your behalf. You still have the pension rights you had built up before leaving, but your eventual pension from the scheme will almost certainly be less than it would have been had you carried on working.

In the case of a money purchase scheme, the pension fund you had built up by the time of leaving continues to be invested and so hopefully grows further between now and retirement. But you have lost the additions to the fund through continuing contributions and the growth that those contributions could have produced.

With a final salary scheme, your eventual pension is reduced because you will have had fewer years in the scheme than if you had stayed until retirement. A further reduction is also likely because the pay on which your pension will be based is the pay at the time you left the scheme and that will usually be a lot lower than your pay would have been had you stayed until retirement. True, the law does require this 'preserved pension' to be increased in line with price inflation between the time you leave and the time you retire, but only up to a maximum 5 per cent a year and prices tend to rise more slowly than earnings. Using the Example on page 228, suppose instead of retiring with average pay of £30,000 and 20 years in the scheme, you had left ten years earlier when your pay was only £21,000. Your preserved pension would initially be 10 × 1/80 × £21,000 = £2,625 a year. If inflation averaged 2.5 per cent a year, this would have increased to £3,360 a year by retirement – a lot less than the £7,500 payable had you stayed until retirement.

You do not have to leave your pension rights in the scheme you have left. You can transfer them to your own personal pension (or, in most cases, to a scheme run by a new employer should you decide to work again at some stage). Particularly where a defined benefit scheme is concerned, whether this is worth doing is a complicated decision which depends crucially on the details of the schemes and plans involved and the assumptions made. You should consider getting professional advice (see 'Further information' on page 239).

Taking a temporary career break

This is likely to reduce your eventual pension.

In a money purchase scheme, no contributions will be paid in while you take the break, so you lose both those payments in and any investment growth they would have produced.

In a final salary scheme, the career break will reduce the number of years you spend in the scheme. Via the pension formula, this will translate into a lower pension. If you intend to go back to working with the same employer, you may be able to get your years of membership before the break and your years after the break treated as continuous. This means that the rules about preserved pensions described above under 'Stopping work altogether without starting your pension' would not apply. So, assuming, you stayed on after the career break until retirement, your whole pension would be based on your pay just before retirement.

When you return to work, you might consider topping up your pension to replace the amount lost because of your career break – see Box overleaf.

Additional voluntary contributions

Under current rules, the most you can pay into an occupational pension scheme is usually 15 per cent of your earnings. Contributions paid by your employer do not count towards this limit.

In practice, most people's regular contributions are typically no more than, say, 5 or 6 per cent of earnings. This gives you plenty of scope to pay in additional amounts voluntarily. These are called 'additional voluntary contributions' (AVCs).

Your employer must offer an AVC scheme that you can use to top up benefits from that employer's pension scheme. Alternatively, you can make free-standing AVCs to a scheme you arrange yourself and which is not linked to a particular occupational scheme.

In addition to the payments above, many people can simultaneously pay up to £3,600 a year (£2,808 after deducting tax relief) into a personal pension. This option is not available if your earnings come to £30,000 or more in the current year and all of the previous five years or if in any of these years you are a 'controlling director' of a company – for example, you are the owner/manager of your own company. These limits on contributions are due to be abolished – see page 239.

Switching to another job or running your own business

As far as the pension from your current employer goes, the position is not unlike stopping work altogether: normally, you cease to be an active member of the scheme but retain the right to receive at retirement, the pension you have built up so far; and, if you choose, you can transfer those rights to another pension scheme or plan. The exceptions are some types of public sector job where, if you transfer to another employer still within the public sector, you might be able to have your years of membership in the old pension scheme transferred and treated as years within the new scheme – your new employer should be able to tell you if this is possible.

If you switch to another employer, check whether it offers an occupational pension scheme. If so, this is likely to be worth joining because you get the benefit of contributions paid in for you by your employer as well as any contributions you yourself pay in.

> 'When I left the Ministry of Defence, I left a good pension scheme, but I am now in the local government scheme which is pretty good as well.'
>
> Harriet

If there is no occupational scheme, unless there are fewer than five employees you should have access to a personal pension through your workplace. This might be either a group personal pension (essentially the same as the personal pensions described below) or a stakeholder pension scheme (see 'Personal pensions' on page 235). Check whether your employer will contribute something to this scheme and, if so, how much.

If you are becoming self-employed (or a partner in a firm), you will have to make your own arrangements to save for retirement – see 'Personal pensions' on page 235.

Reducing the hours you work with your current employer

Cutting the hours you work is likely to involve a reduction in pay which in turn will usually reduce your eventual pension.

In a money purchase scheme, both your own (if the scheme is contributory) and your employer's contributions are usually a percentage of your pay, so the less you earn the smaller the amount paid into your pension scheme and the lower the pension you are likely to get.

In a defined benefit scheme, your pay is one of the factors in the formula used to work out your pension, so lower pay will mean a lower pension.

Taking early retirement or partial retirement

Occupational pension schemes have a normal pension age – often 65 – but you can usually start your pension earlier. At the time of writing, the earliest pension age which the law permits is 50 but this is due to rise to age 55 by 2010. The rules of your own scheme might specify a higher minimum age. (You can start your pension at any age if you have to retire early because of ill health.)

At the time of writing, you cannot start to draw a pension from a scheme run by your current employer while continuing to work as an employee for that same firm. This has always been an anomalous rule because there is nothing to stop you leaving your current job, starting your pension and then also working for someone else. Similarly, you can carry on working while drawing a pension from a former employer's scheme or a personal pension. So it is welcome news that the rule is due to change so that you can draw a pension from your current employer while continuing to work there. This opens the way for a gradual easing back from work, for example, shifting to part-time work while topping up your earnings with a partial pension. So far, the government has not said when this change will be come into effect.

Starting your pension early could be a way to finance, or partially fund, your downshift. But the pension will be lower than if you had waited until the normal retirement age for your scheme.

In a money purchase scheme, the pension fund you have built up is used to buy an annuity or to provide a pension whose amount is based on annuity rates at the time the pension starts. The younger you are when you start your pension, the lower the rate.

In a final salary scheme, your pay at the time you take early retirement is likely to be lower than it would have been had you stayed on until normal retirement age, but that will not always be the case. However, most defined benefit schemes make some reduction (called an 'actuarial reduction') to the amount of pension you get if you decide you want to retire early. Commonly, the reduction is between 4 and 6 per cent for each year you retire early. For example, suppose your final pay was £30,000 and you had been in an 'eightieths scheme' 20 years, your pension would normally be $20 \times 1/80 \times £30,000 = £7,500$ a year. But say you started the pension three years early and the actuarial reduction was 6 per cent a year. Assuming the same earnings, the initial pension would be $17 \times 1/80 \times £30,000 = £6,375$. This would be reduced by $3 \times 6\% = 18\%$ of £6,375, leaving you with a pension of £5,228 a year.

The actuarial reduction might be waived if your employer is seeking redundancies or you retire early because of ill health.

Pensions from occupational schemes must normally be increased each year once they start to be paid, for example, in line with inflation up to a maximum of 2.5 or 5 per cent a year. The rules are complicated and changing so check with your scheme to see how your own pension will be increased. These increases mean that the impact of an actuarial reduction may be fairly rapidly overcome.

Although there is a common legal framework of rules for pensions, they are labyrinthine and there is huge scope for variation from one scheme to another. The only way to plan whether early retirement is a financially viable operation for you is to contact each scheme and ask for a statement showing the pension you could get if you retired now. You then need to check whether this income is likely to continue to be enough as the years progress.

> '*I had belonged to three better-than-average pension schemes for a total of 31 years and so, with lower costs, found I could afford to take early retirement (at age 55½) ... I've heard a lot of people say that they want to retire early but they can't afford to because their pension will be reduced quite severely. Certainly it will be reduced, but you really don't know by how much until you get all the information and do the sums and project them over your expected lifetime – spreadsheets are ideal for this and it's worth investigating different scenarios. You have to ask for an early retirement quotation to find out how much your pension would start at, and the rate at which it will increase (the rules for this may be complicated and different rules may apply to contributions you've made at different periods of time, meaning different portions of your pension are increased at different rates and these may depend on inflation measured over different periods). You have to make assumptions about future inflation.*'
>
> Nick

Personal pensions (including stakeholder schemes)

Personal pensions all work on a money purchase basis. This means the amount of pension you get at retirement depends on:

* the amount paid into the scheme
* how the invested contributions grow
* the amount deducted in charges
* annuity rates at the time you start your pension.

In most cases, you choose whether or not your pension will increase each year once it starts to be paid by buying either a level annuity (no increases) or one with built in increases, for example, 5 per cent a year or in line with inflation. If you choose an increasing annuity, the starting income is lower – see Table 12.5. If (in common with most people) you do opt for a level annuity, it is essential that you consider how you will manage financially later in retirement – see Box. This is especially important where you are starting your pension early and so relying on it to support you for a very long time.

You do not have to be in work or earning to be eligible to pay into a personal pension. Under current rules, nearly everyone can pay at least £3,600 a year (£2,808 a year after deducting tax relief) into personal pensions. If you do have earnings, you can often pay in more.

Table 12.5 Examples of the starting income from different annuities based on a lump sum of £10,000

Type of annuity	Yearly starting income in March 2004		Comment
	Man aged 55	Woman aged 55	
Level annuity	£578	£554	Income does not change from one year to the next, so the buying power of your money falls as prices rise
Annuity increasing by 5 per cent a year	£291	£263	Income increases by 5 per cent each year. If inflation averages more than 5 per cent a year, you still suffer some loss of buying power. If inflation averages less than 5 per cent a year, the buying power of your money increases
RPI-linked annuity	£362	£334	Income rises and falls in line with inflation as measured by the Retail Prices Index (RPI), so its buying power stays the same year after year

Source: Moneyfacts Life & Pensions, average rates

Protecting a fixed income against inflation

Rising prices reduce the buying power of your money. Even low rates of inflation have a big impact on a fixed income over a long period of time. For example, if inflation averaged just 2 per cent a year, £1,000 today would buy only the same as £820 after 10 years and £486 after 20 years. If you take no action to protect yourself against inflation, you risk a big reduction in your standard of living as time goes by.

Pensions from most occupational schemes automatically provide increases each year to at least partially protect you against inflation. But, with most personal pensions, you have to decide whether or not to have this protection.

One way to protect yourself at least partially against inflation is to opt for an increasing annuity that provides an income which rises each year. Or you could choose an RPI-linked annuity where the income rises (and falls) directly in line with inflation, keeping the buying power of the income exactly the same year after year. But there is a price tag to this protection – your starting income from these types of annuity is much lower than the income from a level annuity.

If you have a reasonably large pension fund (or several funds in different plans), you could use just part to buy a level annuity now, leaving the rest invested. You can then use a further part to buy another level annuity later on, and so on. In this way, you gradually increase your pension income.

Another option would be to use your whole pension fund now to buy a level annuity but set aside part of your income to build up savings to boost your income later on.

Stakeholder pensions are personal pensions that meet certain conditions, in particular:

- the only charges must be levied as a percentage of your investment and the maximum charge is 1 per cent a year
- the minimum contribution must be set no higher than £20 (whether as a regular contribution or a lump sum payment)
- you must be allowed to stop and start contributions as you choose without penalty

- you must be able to transfer your pension fund to another pension arrangement without any transfer charges.

Impact of downshifting on your personal pension

Downshifting without starting your pension

Any downshift which involves paying less into your personal pension will reduce your pension compared with what it would otherwise have been.

> '*I had belonged to a pretty good hybrid scheme at work and I left my pension rights to carry on growing in that scheme. Of course, once I left no more contributions were being paid in, so it was important to start my own personal pension. At first, I didn't have any spare cash to do that. But, after a few years, when the business became established, I took out a personal pension (and later transferred to a stakeholder scheme) and have been able to pay in lump sums at irregular intervals. My eventual pension will undoubtedly be lower than it would have been had I stayed in a regular job with a good occupational scheme, but that's a price I'm happy to pay for the life I'm able to lead.'*
>
> Jane

Taking early retirement or partial retirement

At the time of writing, the earliest age at which the law permits you to start drawing your pension is 50 but this is due to rise to age 55 by 2010. The age limit does not apply if you have to retire early because of ill health.

If, for whatever reason, you start to draw your pension early, the pension fund you have built up will be smaller. This is because you lose the later contributions that would have been paid in and you miss out on investment growth between now and a later retirement age. Moreover, annuity rates are lower the younger you are when you buy the annuity. So, not only do you have a smaller pension fund but pound for pound it buys less pension. This loss of pension is permanent and will affect your income throughout retirement.

You'll need to do your sums carefully to check whether you can afford to take an early pension as a way of funding your downshift.

Do this by checking your most recent pension statement(s). Your pension provider must send you a statement each year detailing the size of your pension fund to date and the amount of pension it would buy at current annuity rates.

Changes to the pension rules

From April 2006, the complicated rules about how much you can contribute to different types of pension arrangement are due to be swept away and replaced by a single simplified regime. Under the new regime, you will be able to accumulate pension funds within any number of tax-favoured pension schemes and plans up to a certain value, called the lifetime allowance. Initially, the allowance will be set a £1.5 million and will increase broadly in line with inflation. (A value will be assigned to pension rights from a defined benefit scheme for the purpose of checking against this limit.) In additional, you will have an annual allowance, set initially at £215,000, which will limit the amount by which your pension savings can increase each year through additional contributions or growth in rights. Any amounts over these limits will be taxed at a special rate.

Further information

For information about state pensions generally or your own entitlement, contact The Pension Service★ and, for National Insurance contributions, the Inland Revenue★. If you also belong to an occupational pension scheme or have a personal pension, the statements you get concerning that pension arrangement will be 'combined pension statements' that also include details of the state pension you are likely to get at retirement.

Contact the pensions administrator★ at your workplace to find out about your occupational pension scheme and/or any other pension arrangements available through your workplace.

If you already have a personal pension, your provider can supply details about the plan and the savings you have built up so far. When you want to start taking a pension, your existing pension provider will not necessarily be the best annuity provider, so shop around. You can check out current annuity rates through the FSA

Comparative Tables*, with personal finance publishers such as Moneyfacts* and through independent financial advisers (IFAs) who specialise in annuities*.

If you are shopping around for a personal pension, you can compare what's on offer through the FSA Comparative Tables*. You can contact pension providers direct, but if you would like help choosing, contact one or more IFAs*.

Deciding whether to transfer pension rights from an occupational pension scheme to another scheme or pension arrangement can be complicated. IFAs* can help but check that they have the extra qualifications needed to give this sort of advice. If the value of your pension rights is large, it may be worth paying for help from a consulting actuary* (an independent specialist in areas such as estimating the future value of pensions).

To check that financial advisers and products providers are bona fide and able to offer the type of service you are after, check their authorisation status through the FSA Register*. Provided you deal with an authorised firm, you can be fairly confident that the firm is solvent and conducts its business in a fair manner and you have some protection if things do go wrong, including access to an independent complaints body and compensation scheme.

For more information generally about pensions, see *Planning your Pension* published by Which? Books*.

Addresses

AA (Automobile Association)
Contact Centre
Carr Ellison House
William Armstrong Drive
Newcastle upon Tyne NE4 7YA
Tel: 0870 600 0371
Website: www.theaa.com

Accountant (to find one)
Look in *Yellow Pages* under
'Accountants' or contact the
following professional bodies for
a list of their members in your
area:

- Association of Chartered
  Certified Accountants
  29 Lincoln's Inn Fields
  London WC2A 3EE
  Tel: 020-7396 7000
  Website: www.acca.co.uk
- Institute of Chartered
  Accountants in England and
  Wales
  PO Box 433
  Chartered Accountants' Hall
  Moorgate Place
  London EC2P 2BJ
  Tel: 020-7920 8100
  Website: www.icaew.co.uk

- Institute of Chartered
  Accountants in Ireland
  Chartered Accountants' House
  87–89 Pembroke Road
  Ballsbridge
  Dublin 4
  Republic of Ireland
  Tel: (00353) 1-637 7200
  Website: www.icai.ie
- Institute of Chartered
  Accountants of Scotland
  CA House
  21 Haymarket Yards
  Edinburgh EH12 5BH
  Tel: 0131-347 0100
  Website: www.icas.org.uk

**Association of Policy Market
Makers (APMM)**
The Holywell Centre
1 Phipp Street
London EC2A 4PS
Tel: 020-7739 3949
Website: www.apmm.org

**Association of Tax
Technicians**
12 Upper Belgrave Street
London SW1X 8BB
Tel: 020-7235 2544
Website: www.att.org.uk

Boat Safety Scheme
Willow Grange
Church Road
Watford WD17 4QA
Tel: (01923) 201278
Website:
www.boatsafetyscheme.com

**British Franchise Association
(BFA)**
Thames View
Newtown Road
Henley-on-Thames
Oxfordshire RG9 1HG
Tel: (01491) 578050
Website:
www.british-franchise.org

**British Insurance Brokers'
Association**
14 Bevis Marks
London EC3A 7NT
Tel: 020-7623 9043
Website: www.biba.org.uk

British Waterways
Customer Service Centre
Willow Grange
Church Road
Watford WD17 4QA
Tel: (01923) 201120
Websites:
www.waterwaysnetwork.com,
www.britishwaterways.co.uk

Business Eye
Tel: (08457) 96 97 98
Website:
www.businesseye.org.uk

Business Link
The website contains a lot of
information. To find your local
office, look in *The Phone Book* or
contact as below:
Tel: 0845 600 9 006
Website:
www.businesslink.gov.uk

**Camping and Caravanning
Club**
Greenfields House
Westwood Way
Coventry CV4 8JH
Tel: 024-7669 4995
Website: www.campingand
caravanningclub.co.uk

Canal Junction
Website:
www.canaljunction.com

Careers service
Look in *Yellow Pages* under
'Careers advice' and
'Employment agencies and
consultants'. If you are studying,
your college is likely to have a
service.

**Centre for Alternative
Technology**
Machynlleth
Powys SY20 9AZ
Tel: (01654) 705950
Website: www.cat.org.uk

**Chartered Institute of
Taxation**
12 Upper Belgrave Street
London SW1X 8BB
Tel: 020-7235 9381
Website: www.tax.org.uk

Citizens' Advice Bureau

For local bureau, see *The Phone Book* or the website:
www.citizensadvice.org.uk
Website for online information:
www.adviceguide.org.uk

Clear Skies

BRE Ltd
Building 17
Garston
Watford WD25 9XX
Tel: 0870 243 0930
Website: www.clear-skies.org

Commission for Racial Equality

St Dunstan's House
201–211 Borough High Street
London SE1 1GZ
Tel: 020-7939 0000
Website:www.cre.gov.uk

Community Legal Service

For lawyers and advice centres in your area (England and Wales only) able to help with, for example, debt problems and landlord-tenant disputes:
Tel: 0845 608 1122
Website: www.justask.org.uk

Companies House

- Crown Way, Maindy, Cardiff CF14 3UZ
- 37 Castel Terrace, Edinburgh EH1 2EB
- 21 Bloomsbury Street, London WC1B 3XD

Tel: 0870 333 3636
Website:
www.companieshouse.gov.uk

Consulting actuary

- Association of Consulting Actuaries
  1 Wardrobe Place
  London EC4V 5AG
  Tel: 020-7248 3163
  Website: www.aca.org.uk
- Society of Pension Consultants
  St Bartholomew House
  92 Fleet Street
  London EC4Y 1DG
  Tel: 020-7353 1688
  Website: www.spc.uk.com

Consumer Credit Counselling Service (CCCS)

Wade House
Merrion Centre
Leeds LS2 8NG
Tel: 0800 138 1111
Website: www.cccs.co.uk

Council of Mortgage Lenders (CML)

3 Savile Row
London W1S 3PB
Tel: 020-7440 2255
Website: www.cml.org.uk

Department for Education and Skills (DfES)

Sanctuary Buildings
Great Smith Street
London SW1P 3BT
Tel: information line (student finance): 0800 731 9133
Website: www.dfes.gov.uk/studentsupport

**Department for Employment
and Learning Northern
Ireland (Student Support
Branch)**
Adelaide House
39–49 Adelaide Street
Belfast BT2 8FD
Tel: 028-9025 7710
Websites: www.delni.gov.uk,
www.delni.gov.uk/
studentsupport

**Department for Work and
Pensions**
Contact your local Jobcentre
Plus (if you are of working age)
or the Pension Service (if you are
over state pension age or your
enquiry concerns pensions) –
see separate entries below.
Tel: 020-7712 2171
Website: www.dwp.gov.uk

Department of Health
For information about financial
help available for students on
health-related courses:
PO Box 777
London SE1 6XH
Tel: 08701 555 455
Website:
www.doh.gov.uk/hcsmain.htm

**Department of Trade and
Industry (DTI)**
Tel: 020-7215 5000
Websites: www.dti.gov.uk,
www.tiger.gov.uk (Tailored
Interactive Guidance on
Employment Rights),
www.dti.gov.uk/cgi-bin/wlb
(work–life balance)

Diggers & Dreamers
Website:
www.diggersanddreamers.org.uk

Direct Marketing Association
DMA House
70 Margaret Street
London W1W 8SS
Tel: 020-7291 3300
Website: www.dma.org.uk

**Direct Selling Association
(DSA)**
29 Floral Street
London WC2E 9DP
Tel: 020-7497 1234
Website: http://194.203.128.226

Disability Rights Commission
DRC Helpline
Freepost MID02164
Stratford-upon-Avon CV37 9BR
Tel: 08457 622 633
Website: www.drc-gb.org

Doing Your Bit
Website:
www.doingyourbit.org.uk

Employment tribunal
To find your nearest tribunal,
see phone book or contact:
Tel: 0845 795 9775
Website:
www.employmenttribunals.gov.uk

**Energy supplier comparison
websites**
Websites: www.unravelit.com,
www.uswitch.com

Energywatch

To find your local office, contact:
Tel: 08459 06 07 08
Website:
www.energywatch.org.uk

Environment Agency

To find your local office,
see *The Phone Book* or call the
enquiry line:
General Enquiry Line:
Tel: 0845 9333111
Website: www.environment-
agency.gov.uk

Equal Opportunities Commission (EOC)

Arndale House
Arndale Centre
Manchester M4 3EQ
Tel: 0845 601 5901
Website: www.eoc.org.uk

Findhorn

The Findhorn Foundation
The Park
Findhorn
Moray IV36 3TZ
Tel: (01309) 690311
Website: www.findhorn.org

FSA Comparative Tables

Tel: 0845 606 1234
Website: www.fsa.gov.uk/tables

FSA Register

Tel: 0845 606 1234
Website: www.fsa.gov.uk/
consumer (follow link to Firm
and Person Check Service)

General Social Care Council

Bursaries Office
Goldings House
2 Hay's Lane
London SE1 2HB
Tel: 020-7397 5835
Website: www.gscc.org.uk

Health and Safety Executive

HSE Infoline
Caerphilly Business Park
Caerphilly CF83 3GG
Tel: 08701 545500
Website: www.hse.gov.uk

Higher Education & Research Opportunities in the United Kingdom (HERO)

Website: www.hero.ac.uk

Highlands and Islands Enterprise

Cowan House
Inverness Retail and Business
Park
Inverness
IV2 7GF
Tel: 01463 234171
Website: hie.co.uk

Housing advice centre

Run by your local your district,
borough, unitary or metropolitan
council authority. See *The Phone
Book* under the name of your
council.

IFA Promotion

*For a list of IFAs in your area,
contact:*
Tel: 0800 085 3250
Website: www.unbiased.co.uk

Independent financial adviser (IFA)

To find an IFA see separate entries for the following organisations:

- IFA Promotion
- The Institute of Financial Planning
- Matrix Data UK IFA Directory
- Society of Financial Advisers (SOFA)

Independent financial advisers (IFAs) who specialise in annuities

- The Annuity Bureau
  The Tower
  11 York Road
  London SE1 7NX
  Tel: 0845 602 6263
  Website:
  www.bureauxltd.com
- Annuity Direct
  32 Scrutton Street
  London EC2A 4RQ
  Tel: 0500 506575
  Website:
  www.annuitydirect.co.uk
- Hargreaves Lansdown
  Annuity Supermarket
  Website:
  www.hargreaveslansdown.
  co.uk/pensions
- WBA Ltd
  Tel: 020-7421 4545
  Website:
  www.williamburrows.com

Inland Revenue

For local tax enquiry centres look in *The Phone Book* under 'Inland Revenue'.
Website:
www.inlandrevenue.gov.uk

Institute of Financial Planning

Whitefriars Centre
Lewins Mead
Bristol BS1 2NT
Tel: 0117-945 2470
Website:
www.financialplanning.org.uk

Insurance broker

- Look in *The Phone Book* under 'Insurance – Intermediaries'.
- For members of the General Insurance Standards Council:
  110 Cannon Street
  London EC4N 6EU
  Tel: 020-7648 7810
  Website: www.gisc.co.uk
- From 14 January 2005, insurance intermediaries will be regulated by the Financial Services Authority – check an intermediary is authorised by contacting the FSA Register (see above).

Invest Northern Ireland

44–58 May Street
Belfast BT1 4NN
Tel: 028-9023 9090
Website: www.investni.com

Jobcentre Plus
For your local office, check the website or see *The Phone Book*.
Website:
www.jobcentreplus.gov.uk

LearnDirect
Website:
www.learndirect-advice.co.uk

Leisure and Living: Parks
Website: www.martex.co.uk/leisure-and-living

Letslink UK
12 Southcote Road
London N19 5BJ
Tel: 020-7607 7852
Website: www.letslinkuk.net

Lifelong Learning
Website:
www.lifelonglearning.co.uk
Website for information about career development loans: www.lifelonglearning.dfes.gov.uk/cdl

Local authority
See *The Phone Book* under the name of your local authority.

Local Education Authority (LEA) (England and Wales)
See *The Phone Book* under the name of your local authority.
You can also find a list of LEA contacts at these websites:
www.dfes.gov.uk/studentsupport
For publications about student finance, tel: 0800 731 9133
For detailed questions about student finance and eligibility, tel: (01325) 392822
Website:
www.studentfinancedirect.co.uk

Local employment agencies
Look in *Yellow Pages* under 'Employment agencies'.

Local planning authority
See *The Phone Book* under the name of your local authority.

Matrix Data UK IFA Directory
Website:
www.ukifadirectory.co.uk

Moneyfacts
Larger public reference libraries may have copies.
Tel: 0870 2250 100
(subscriptions)
Website: www.moneyfacts.co.uk

Mortgage broker
- See *The Phone Book* under 'Mortgages'
- For intermediaries that abide by the Mortgage Code: Mortgage Code Compliance Board (MCCB) University Court Stafford ST18 0GN Tel: (01785) 218 200 Website: www.mortgagecode.org.uk
- From 31 October 2004, mortgage intermediaries will be regulated by the Financial Services Authority – check an intermediary is authorised by contacting the FSA Register (see above).

National Association of Boat Owners (NABO)
Freepost (BM8367)
Birmingham B31 2BR
Website:www.nabo.org.uk

National Debtline
Tel: 0808 808 4000
Website:
www.nationaldebtline.co.uk

National Park Homes Council (NPHC)
Catherine House
Victoria Road
Aldershot
Hants GU11 1SS
Tel: (01252) 336092
Website: www.theparkhome.net

NHS Wales Student Awards Unit
2nd Floor
Golate House
101 St Mary Street
Cardiff CF10 1DX.
Tel: 029-2026 1495

Office of the Deputy Prime Minister (ODPM)
ODPM Free Literature
PO Box 236
Wetherby LS23 7NB
Tel: 0870 1226 236
Website:www.odpm.gov.uk

Open University (OU)
To find your nearest OU Regional Centre, use the website or look in *The Phone Book*.
Website: www3.open.ac.uk

Patent Office
Concept House
Cardiff Road
Newport
NP10 8QQ
Tel: 0845 950 0505
Website: www.patent.gov.uk

Pension Schemes Registry
PO Box 1NN
Newcastle upon Tyne
NE99 1NN
Tel: 0191-225 6316
Website:
www.opra.gov.uk/traceAPension

Pension Service, The
For local office, check website or see *The Phone Book*.
Website:
www.thepensionservice.gov.uk

Pensions administrator (occupational pension scheme)
Usually located in your Human Resources (Personnel) Department. Contact details will also be in any booklet and correspondence about the scheme and on any pensions notice board at work.

Personal finance magazines
Check out newsagents and larger public libraries.

Personal finance pages of newspapers
As a rough guide, usually in the Wednesday edition of tabloids, Saturday edition of broadsheets and most Sunday papers.

Personal finance websites

There are many of these.
Useful sites include:
http://news.ft.com/yourmoney,
www.moneyextra.com.
www.moneysupermarket.com

Quality Award Parks

Website:
www.qualityawardparks.co.uk

Residential Boat Owners' Association (RBOA)

PO Box 518
Rickmansworth
London WD3 1WJ
Website: www.rboa.org.uk

Residential Landlords Association

1 Roebuck Lane
Sale
Manchester M33 7SY
Tel: 0845 666 5000
Website: www.rla.org.uk

Royal Yachting Association (RYA)

RYA House
Ensign Way
Hamble
Southampton SO31 4YA
Tel: 0845 345 0400
Website: www.rya.org.uk

Save-a-Flush

KMA (UK) Ltd
62 Stockport Road
Cheadle
Cheshire SK8 2AF
Website: www.save-a-flush.co.uk

Save Energy

Energy Efficiency Helpline:
0845 727 7200
Website: www.saveenergy.co.uk

Scottish Enterprise

5 Atlantic Quay
150 Broomielaw
Glasgow G2 8LU
Tel: 0845 607 8787
Website:
www.scottish-enterprise.com

Shelterline

See *The Phone Book* or use
contact details below to find your
local Shelter Housing Aid
Centre.
Tel: 0808 800 4444
Website: www.shelter.org.uk

Sheriff Court (Scotland)

To find your nearest court, look
in *The Phone Book* under 'Courts'
or check the website:
Website:
www.scotcourts.gov.uk/html/
sheriff.htm

Society of Financial Advisers (SOFA)

For a list of independent
financial advisers who all have
more than just the basic
qualifications, contact:
20 Aldermanbury
London EC2V 7HY
Tel: 020-8989 8464
Website: www.sofa.org

Solicitor

Look in *Yellow Pages* under 'Solicitors' or contact the following professional bodies for a list of their members in your area:

- Law Society
  113 Chancery Lane
  London WC2A 1PL
  Tel: 020-7242 1222
  Website:
  www.lawsociety.org.uk
- Law Society of Scotland
  26 Drumsheugh Gardens
  Edinburgh EH3 7YR
  Tel: 0131-226 7411
  Website: www.lawscot.org.uk
- Law Society of Northern Ireland
  98 Victoria Street
  Belfast BT1 3JZ
  Tel: 028-90 231614
  Website: www.lawsoc-ni.org

Student Awards Agency for Scotland

Tel: 0131-476 8212
Website: www.student-support-saas.gov.uk

Student Loans Company

100 Bothwell Street
Glasgow G2 7JD
Tel: 0870 24 23 22 0
Website: www.slc.co.uk

Switch with Which?

Website:
www.switchwithwhich.co.uk

Teaching Information Line (England and Wales)

Tel: 0845 6000 991; (Welsh language) 0845 6000 992.
Website:
www.useyourheadteach.gov.uk

Trading Standards Department

To find your local office, see *The Phone Book* under entry for your local authority.
Website:
www.tradingstandards.gov.uk

Universities and Colleges Admissions Service (UCAS)

Website: www.ucas.ac.uk

Which? and Which? Books

Freepost
PO 44
Hertford X
SG14 1YB
Tel: 0800 252 100
Website: www.which.net

Index